Praise God
He Knew
The Troubles I'd See

Nancy J. Stoll

First Edition

Some names and identifying details have been changed to protect the privacy of individuals.

ISBN: 979-8-9869196-2-1
ISBN: 979-8-9869196-3-8 (e-book)

Publishing Consultant: Yo Productions LLC (yoproductions.net)

Cover Design: David Sanders Jr.

Printed in the United States

TRIBUTE AND DEDICATION

This, my second book, is lovingly dedicated to and in memory of a wonderful Christian woman, Obieray (Obie) Rogers, who helped me with my first book. From day one, I thought of her as the Christ-centered helpmate and "midwife" God had sent to me to help me "birth" my first book. She served as my editor, publishing guide, and taught me all the things I needed to know to bring my first book, *Praise God He Knew I Was a Slow Learner*, to life. And believe me, there was a lot more to it than writing the book!

Obie and I spent many hours together throughout 2022 and into early 2023, but we never met face-to-face. Our time together was always spent via the internet, emails, or over the phone. I regret that deeply to this very day, for she passed away in July 2023. I never had the opportunity to hug her and thank her in person for all she did for me.

However, I did attend her "Service of Triumph" funeral service at the church she had faithfully attended and actively served for many years, in various capacities. And, let me tell you, if you want to gain great insight into what kind of person someone was in life, attending their church funeral service is a great way to do so.

Obie was a loving, dedicated servant of the Lord within her

church and community. She had retired after working for the City of Columbus for thirty years. She owned and operated her own publishing company, held a passion for writing, and had authored many books focused on God's love and growing stronger in our faith walk with Him. And she gave God the praise and glory for it all. She was greatly loved and respected by her family and all who knew her.

I walked out of that service feeling as though I knew her well.

Obie, someday we're going to meet face-to-face in Heaven, and I'm going to give you a big, loving Heavenly hug of thanks as we together give God the glory for it all!

Obie, thank you for being you and an important person in my life!

TABLE OF CONTENTS

PROLOGUE

This prodigal daughter had returned home to a state that she had once sworn to God she'd never return to—her home state of Ohio. Yes, God had brought me back home, and I was joyfully grateful for it too. I was leaving my past behind.

Prayers of great gratitude were being uplifted to God for He had loved and taken care of me throughout my entire life through:

- A failed marriage and becoming a single parent.
- Tumultuous, potentially detrimental, and heartbreaking personal relationships.
- A stressful yet rewarding multi-state career in corporate retail, small business development, as well as community and state economic development.
- The loss of my home and possessions in a fire set by the thieves.
- The unexpected elimination of my Texas State Chamber position.

And now, God had opened doors to a career opportunity that seemed to have been designed specifically for me and was now awaiting me in Columbus, Ohio.

It was almost unbelievable. It felt almost impossible. "But God" (two of my favorite words in the Bible) worked it all for my good!

Through it all, God taught me some mighty hard yet amazing life and spiritual growth lessons. I praised Him for all of them because I was now applying what I had learned to my life.

However, the greatest praise was for how He had turned me around! I was becoming a new person in Him!

After forty years of thinking I was in control of my life—being a "Jacob," and a "Jonah"—God helped me realize two most important things: my plan was not the best, and my "I, Me, My, Mine, I can do all things through Me, Myself, and I" attitude had only messed up my life. He led me to realize that total submission to Him and His ways were the best. All He ever wanted was His "best-ever" life for me, which He had planned before I was born!

My life immediately started to change for the better the moment I gave up control and surrendered everything to God. He opened doors that no one could shut. He led me to the almost perfectly designed *"just for me"* leadership position in my home state of Ohio. Plus, He had assured in unbelievable ways that all my financial worries were washed away. Life was good. I thought my troubles were behind me. However, if you think, as I did, that by totally surrendering everything to the Lord and asking Him to take control, I would live a life without any pain, problems, pitfalls, trials, and troubles, you would be wrong! Nope, Jesus was right when He told his disciple in John 16:33, "In this world, you will have trouble." Yep, He was right. My troubles were not over. Major painful lessons awaited me.

God wasn't done teaching me. However, the subject matter of lessons would change. They would center on the challenging and difficult task of renewing my human mind to align with His, modeling my life after Jesus's examples, and strengthening my faith-walk with Him. All these lessons were designed to accomplish three things: (1) reinforce my loving faith walk in Him, (2) prove that He always keeps His promises; and (3) develop and establish deep within me a strong, "I will trust God in all things—No Matter What" attitude and outlook on life.

Turn the page! My almost unbelievable but true-life stories of learning how to renew my mind and, no matter what, trust Him in the face of troubles, trials, pain, pitfalls, and even the fear of being killed await you.

It is my greatest hope and prayer that as you read this book, your faith walk with Him and your ability to trust Him in all things "No Matter What" will be ignited, empowered, and become stronger. And as it does, may you experience the incredible greatness of God's power in your life when you believe, obey, and trust in Him.

Come along with me now as I share the lessons God taught me in renewing my mind and trusting Him, no matter our circumstances. This type of trust is truly the deepest and strongest level of faith that God wants you to grow into. God encourages and invites us to take Him at his word, for John 15:7 says, "If you remain in me and my words remain in you, ask whatever you wish, and it will be done for you." He did it for me. He can and will do it for you.

~ 1 ~
NEW BEGINNINGS, OLD TRAITS

It was a beautiful fall morning in Columbus, Ohio. The sun poured through the windows, and I felt its warmth envelop me. It was going to be a wonderful day. A new, vibrant life awaited me. Major changes had already occurred in my life, and more were about to come. I knew this for three reasons.

The first was the realization that God's forgiveness, grace, and unconditional love had sustained me throughout my troubled past. Next was experiencing the unbelievable yet real miracles God had recently done in my life. The final reason was that I now also understood the meanings of the words *sanctification, transformation, renewing of my mind,* and *what people meant when they had said I had to "die to self."*

Believe me, when I accepted Christ at the age of seven, I didn't understand any of these words, and the thought of having to "die to self" because that's what my Pastor said I had to do, scared me half to death! However, after forty years, I finally understood that the phrase simply meant, as 2 Corinthians 5:14-15 (NLT) explains, "Christ's love controls us. Since we believe that Christ died for all, we also believe that we have all died to our old life. He died for everyone so that those who receive his new life will no longer live for themselves. Instead, they will live for Christ, who died and was raised for them."

I had to put His desires, not mine, first in my life and live my life for Him. Sanctification and transformation meant I needed to become more like Jesus in all I did. Renewing my mind meant I had to change my worldly self-centered "I, Me, My, Mine, I can do all things through Me, Myself, and I" mindset and realize that God is God, I am not. With that knowledge bubbling in my brain, my desire to make all those tasks happen was strong.

Thoughts of past years floated way back to several days after graduating from college. I was silently thanking God for the beautiful Christian parents He had blessed me with, for the life I had led, and for the opportunities that lay ahead. However, that was immediately followed by saying, "But Lord! You screwed up in one major way. You had me born and raised in the wrong part of the country! Northwest Ohio is too gray, too flat, and way too cold. You know I seriously dislike winter weather."

Therefore, my sworn future goal was to someday leave Ohio and never return. And thanks to my controlling mindset, that was exactly what I made happen. And over the years to come, that mindset had only grown stronger.

However, now quietly setting in the Ohio sun rays, I joyfully prayed, "Lord, through it all, you have taken care of me, loved me, and worked all things for my good. You've proven that you are God, and I am not. I'm going to try my best to leave my 'I, Me, My, Mine, I can do all things through Me, Myself, and I' mindset behind. You are in control. The only way I can do anything is through Christ, who strengthens me."

I then paused in my prayer, chuckled, and added, "Oh, and Lord, you've also proven three other things. You never screw up. You do have a sense of humor. And the old cliché of 'Never say never to God' isn't a cliché. It's the truth!"

I lived outside of Ohio for fifteen years. However, only two months ago, I desperately pleaded with God to get me out of Texas, help me find a new, purpose-filled job, and show me where "home" was. And, without question, He did!

He opened doors no human could shut and brought me back home to Ohio. He opened my eyes to see how He had taken my entire trouble-filled past, along with all my terrible controlling choices, and turned them all into a new life living with Him back in the State I swore that I would never live in again. Yes, God had worked His miracles. A new life was beginning in both my natural and spiritual worlds.

My position with the Central Ohio Small Business Development Center (COSBDC) would start the Monday after Thanksgiving.

Tons of things needed to be done, and time was of the essence. Therefore, being a task-oriented person, a to-do list was created.

The last thing on the list was to go shopping. There were two things I wasn't looking forward to purchasing: a winter coat and a pair of snow boots. However, the top three tasks were as follows:

1. Find a place of my own to live. Jo, my twin sister, and her husband, Ken, had graciously welcomed me to live with them until I secured a place of my own. Don't get me wrong, I was thankful for their loving willingness to let me stay with them. But I wanted my own place, and there was no way I wanted to move after starting a new job or during any part of Ohio's winter months.
2. Find a new home church where I would feel like a part of the family of God and in which its pastor was not only ordained by man but also anointed by God. He had to have his ears and heart attuned to God. And because of this, I would be fed well from the Word of God and grow in my faith walk with the Lord.
3. I needed to spend time with my immediate family and rekindle a loving relationship with them. This item was extremely important to me. I knew it would take time because I hadn't desired to truly connect with them for years. I needed to spend time with Jo. I wanted to spend time with my parents, who lived in Northwest Ohio. I also wanted to visit with my youngest

sister, Jodie. She and her husband lived in the Columbus area and were expecting their first child. Matter of fact, Jodie swore the reason God brought me back to Ohio was so I could share this event with her.

The driven desire to share and spend time with all of them was spurred by two reasons. I deeply and sincerely loved each one of them. Plus, I wanted them to experience and realize how God was changing me from the inside out. I wanted them to see how He was working to turn me into the person He had designed for me to become.

Given this, I especially wanted to rekindle the loving Christ-centered twin sister relationship Jo and I once had. I knew this wouldn't happen overnight. Over the years, our relationship had deteriorated. During my self-centered, troubled past, I knowingly and unknowingly had hurt and troubled her deeply. I needed to ask for her forgiveness. My desire to have her see that God was working on renewing my life, my mind, faith, and trust in Him was strong. It was so strong that I could almost taste it. It was like Psalm 34:8 had come alive within me, and I wanted to shout it out, "Oh, taste and see that the Lord *is* good; Blessed is the man who trusts in Him!" (NKJV).

This last desire took a lot of time. I often felt how the Old Testament's Jacob must have felt after God had blessed, changed him, and given him a new name, Israel. In the past, Jacob had wronged his twin brother, Esau, on numerous occasions. He had even deceitfully stolen his birthright from him. They had not seen each other in years, and when they reconnected, Esau looked at his twin brother and simply said, "Jacob." Now being a new person in God's eyes, Jacob replied, more or less, "I'm not who I was. I am not that person anymore." (This full encounter is found in Genesis 33.)

Many times, I said almost that very thing to Jo. I would ask for her forgiveness and beg her to "stop hitting the rewind button into our past because God had erased it all. I'm not who I was!" However, after many weeks of shared experiences and consistently maintaining my attitude, words, and actions, it happened! Here's the event that finally disintegrated the "rewind button."

It was shortly after finalizing my lease agreement to live in a townhouse located about a mile from Jo and Ken. My new landlord, who lived in the townhouse adjacent to mine, was extremely happy to have me as his new tenant.

Two days after signing the lease agreement, movers unloaded everything I had into my new home and positioned it all where I had directed. However, I was very unwise in telling them what to do with several things that should have been taken upstairs. Two of those things included the heavy cannonball bed frame and its queen-size mattress. I merely directed them to lean them both against the wall in the first-floor family room.

By the end of the evening, most of the main floor cleaning and unpacking were done. I was tired and decided to go back to Jo and Ken's. I'd move my bedroom furniture upstairs tomorrow morning.

Tomorrow came. My goal was to finish cleaning and unpacking the main floor. Once that was finished, I'd tackle cleaning the second floor and move the bed frame and mattress to what would be my bedroom. Things were going well, and it was finally time to move the bedframe and mattress upstairs.

That is when the world seemed to come crashing down around me. I couldn't get the mattress up the stairs. For almost two hours, I tried everything, but nothing worked because of the beveled ceiling at the bottom of the stairway and the sharp left turn required.

With tears flowing down my face, I slumped to the floor and desperately and quite frantically cried, "Lord, what am I going to do? I spent tons of money on this bed and mattress, and now I can't get it upstairs. Who knows, maybe even the bed frame won't go up either. Lord, I refuse to have my bedroom in the downstairs living or family room. I want it in my bedroom! I've signed the lease and paid tons of money to live here. Now, I can't get the mattress up the stairs. Can I even live here? If I decide I can't, will the landlord let me out of the lease and refund all my money?"

I sat on the couch feeling defeated. Many tears rolled down my face as many other what-if concerns flowed through my mind. However, I abruptly stopped. I stood up, took a deep breath, bowed my head, lifted my palms to heaven, and said, "Lord, forgive me. You have taught me not to worry, and right now, this is feeling a lot like worry." And as I shook my hands, I said, "Here, Lord, you take this. I've tried to make it happen, but I can't. I give it to you! Help me, please." And with that, I locked up the house, hopped into my car, and headed back to Jo and Ken's.

As I sat at the stoplight at the end of the block, who should turn onto the block but my landlord himself. He stopped, rolled down his window, and with a big smile asked, "How's the move going?" I immediately took the opportunity to tell him all about my problems.

His response was quite unexpected and most positive. He advised that he would call his friend, who was our backdoor neighbor, to see if, together, they could make it happen. He told me he'd get back to me later that night with their plan of action. What he said next astounded me. He told me that if all efforts failed, he didn't care what needed to happen to restructure the stairway. He would make it happen. He wanted me as his tenant and wanted me to make the townhouse my home.

Ya wanna talk about frustrations and troubles turning into joyful praises to God? That's what was happening in my car as I drove back to Jo and Ken's. I knew God was teaching me, once again, not to worry but instead give it to Him. I couldn't wait to tell Jo about the whole thing.

Jo was working in her flower beds as I pulled into the drive. I jumped out of my car and yelled, "Jo, you won't believe what just happened!" A concerned look crossed her face, but it would soon be replaced with a look of pure joy. Ken joined us as I shared my day's report. By the time I had covered everything, all of us were joyfully celebrating in the Lord.

My new landlord called later and advised me to meet him and his friend, George, at the townhouse the next day at 5:00 p.m. I went to bed that night resting assured that God had the whole situation in His hands.

The next day came. There was no way I wanted to walk into and face the troubled environment of the townhouse by myself. I wasn't ready for it yet. Therefore, I busied myself and went shopping for the dreaded winter boots and heavy winter coat I needed. I wanted to check those items off my list.

Arriving promptly at 5:00 p.m. I found no one there, and the front door was still locked. My landlord's car wasn't even in his driveway. What was up with that? I went back to my car and sat waiting for someone to show up. However, no one did. After a while, I decided to go inside and see if I could, once again, try and get the mattress moved upstairs.

Entering the townhouse, nothing looked out of place. However, I abruptly stopped as I turned into the family room to start moving the frame and mattress. The bed frame and queen-size mattress were gone. Hoping my landlord had moved them, I frantically checked every inch of the main floor and the garage. They were nowhere to be found! They were gone! Fear, worry, and despair overtook my thoughts as I sank onto the living room couch. Had someone broken into my home and stolen my stuff just like they had done in Texas?

I started to cry, praying to God, saying, "Lord, help me. I need You now! This can't be happening again. I've looked everywhere, but they aren't here." That is when I heard a quiet thought inside me say, *Oh, Nancy, look around you. Your TV and stereo system are still here. Have you really looked everywhere? You haven't looked upstairs.* Of course, my mental response to that was, "Yes, I have looked everywhere. I couldn't get it upstairs last night, so how could it all be up there now?" To which I heard this reply, *Be still and know that I am God. Go look upstairs.*

I begrudgingly got up and went upstairs. As I opened the bedroom door, there it was! Not only were the bed frame and mattress in my room, but they were set up exactly where I wanted them. I stood there totally amazed, wondering how in the world this could have happened. Both my landlord and George had to work that day.

Just then, the doorbell rang. It was my landlord and his friend George coming to let me know that they had both gotten off work early and had come over earlier to tackle the feat. The move and setup were completed within an hour by removing the front entrance door from its hinges. All I had to do now was make the bed! As sincere thanks were expressed to them, my mind was also shouting gracious praises to God. He had, once again, proven that He was God. He had gone before me to handle it all. My spirit was rejoicing in Him.

Immediately after they left, I headed back to Jo's. I was thrilled half to death and couldn't wait to tell her all about what had just happened.

One of my mother's favorite gospel songs, "Why Should I Worry or Fret," came to mind, and I began to sing it as I drove. The song was written by Doug Oldham in 1968 and released by Sony Music Entertainment in 1970. It speaks of the assurance you can have when you know God holds your future in the palms of His hands. You don't have to worry or fret about anything when you know and believe that God is in control. He holds it all in His hands because you are a part of His almighty plan. Oh, I sang that song loud and strong.

Jo was in the backyard when I arrived. Eagerly and excitedly jumping out of the car, I yelled, "Jo, you won't believe what just happened!" Her face first showed concern. However, a wonderfully warm, beaming smile began to spread across her face as all the details of the past two hours poured out of me. Once again, we were both rejoicing in the Lord by the end of my eventful praise report. And that's when it happened!

Jo looked at me and said, "Wow, Nancy, you have changed! You used to be the most negative and angry worrywart in the world. You've changed! You truly are not who you used to be. God is renewing every part of you!" Her comments were immediately followed by lots of loving hugs and rejoicing in the Lord together. Together, God and I had won this battle of "used-to-bes."

The move was completed, and I happily settled into my new home by late October 1999. Much of my task list had been completed by that time as well. Therefore, my nights at home were quietly spent and filled with thoughts of close personal friends I'd left behind in Arkansas and Texas.

I had not yet made many personal friends. My closest and dearest "friends" were presently my family members. I was definitely missing that close, almost family-like, personal friendship in which I could also share my joys and deepest personal concerns.

I missed Sue and Ben, and the caring friendship we'd shared in Arkansas. They had figuratively adopted Elizabeth and me into their family. Sue and I were like "sisters from another mother." We had shared so much of our lives while I lived in Arkansas. I was lonely and missed them terribly. With that strong thought in my mind, I picked up the phone and called Sue.

By the end of the call, I had accepted her invitation to join them in celebrating their "Early Thanksgiving Holiday" weekend. Her entire family would be gathering at her house the weekend prior to Thanksgiving. It would be like a grand family reunion yet allow individual families to then celebrate the actual holiday the following weekend.

It was perfect! I could go see them all, spend the weekend with them, and still be home in Ohio to celebrate the actual Thanksgiving with my family. I was so excited! I couldn't wait to see them all again!

Little did I know, during that weekend, I would fail an important test God would give me. I would become my own worst enemy.

Words of Wisdom: *There are several essential things you must do if you have recently accepted Christ or if you desire to* *strengthen or restore a life living in Him. Renew your mind and become an apprentice of the Lord Jesus Christ! He was and is the greatest example and Mentor one could ever have to follow. God sent Him to set the examples we should follow. Get into the Word of God and find out how Jesus lived His life from its beginning to its end. As His apprentice, Jesus will lovingly mentor and teach you through the examples He provides in the Bible. The Bible is the greatest instruction manual ever written! Believe and learn from what His Word tells you. Then, as James 1:22a (KJV) says, "Be doers of the Word and not hearers only." Put it into action! Model what Jesus did and how He handled things. Intentionally and consistently model Him within your life. Yet know it is going to be tough sometimes because the daily battle of renewing your mind will always be "In your mind!" The devil will never give up trying to make your efforts fail. Therefore, never give up on Jesus when life gets tough. Run to Him, cling to Him, and ask Him to take control. He will hear your cry and answer you. He'll be with you and mentor you through it. Spend time talking with Him and immerse yourself in the Word of God. He will strengthen you and your efforts to become strong in Him. However, as you'll soon see in my life and being "human" as we all are, this may prove to be easier said than done.*

~ 2 ~
PERILOUS POWERS OF THE MIND

The cross-country drive to Arkansas was beautiful. The remnant of God sprinkling His colorful box of Trix cereal over the treed landscape was still visible.

Sue and Ben had moved and now lived in a small, two-bedroom home located in the rural hinterlands of Arkansas. Their directions made the trip almost trouble-free, and the joy of seeing them heightened with every mile.

However, as I turned onto the road leading back to their wooded country home, I remembered that Arkansas "outback" roads weren't like subdivision side streets in Ohio. They are bumpy, hilly, rough, rocky, and rugged dirt paths.

My Eagle Talon low-ride sports car didn't like them, nor did I. Prayers of "Oh Lord, please don't let my car bottom out!" were said repeatedly as I traveled the last two miles. But my emotions changed the minute I saw Sue running out to greet me, with Ben not far behind. Warm, loving hugs were shared by all.

Surprisingly, Sue's daughter greeted me at the door with a hug. Her family had come a day early to help with the Thanksgiving preparations. Sue quietly apologized and informed me that her daughter and family were planning to stay the entire weekend. Therefore, the spare bedroom had been given to them. I would be sleeping on the living room couch. I assured Sue, there's no need to apologize by saying, "My suitcase is small and I'm so short I've proven many times I can sprawl out on a loveseat and sleep quite comfortably." We both laughed as we entered the small kitchen, which was jammed with food waiting to be prepared.

An hour later, a handsome man walked in the front door and announced, "I'm home!" Who was this man? I had never met him at any of their numerous family gatherings. In my eyes, he looked like a younger, dark-haired, extremely good-looking version of a "Bad Boy, Billy Bob Thornton." Sue introduced her relative, Doug, and added that he had recently been released from prison, was temporarily staying in their camper behind the house, and was looking forward to starting a new life.

The words that stuck in my head were "looking forward to starting a new life." However, I quickly and willingly chose to disregard the "just released from prison" part of her statement. He wanted to start a new life. I knew how that felt. My interest piqued, and I soon let 2 Corinthians 10:5b fall to the floor. That Scripture tells us to take captive every one of our thoughts to make them obedient to Christ. My thoughts were not, in any way, those that would make me obedient to Christ. Instead, my mind and behavior toward Doug started to imitate the world, and I would soon become my own worst enemy.

Doug and I spent a lot of time talking and getting to know each other better as the days progressed. His name still sounded familiar, but, outside of the word *crazy*, I couldn't clearly remember exactly what anyone in the past had said about him. He didn't look or act crazy to me. To me, he came across as good-humored and happy. He seemed like a nice, caring guy who had a lot of personal desires. Sure, some people angered, irritated, and frustrated him, but I chose to blow those comments to the wind, saying, "Doug, you're not alone. We all have those types of people and situations in our lives." My opinion of him was quite positive by the time he called it a night and went to the camper.

As he left, Sue pulled me aside and said, "Girl, we need to talk. Come with me." Shutting her bedroom door, she turned with a concerned look and asked, "Nancy, what the heck are you doing?" Her question confused me. Sue had experienced me chumming up with a guy before. Why should I have to explain my behavior to her?

Sue, frustratingly, looked at me and asked, "Don't you remember anything anyone has said about him?"

I responded, "No, not really. I do remember he was in jail, but I have no idea why. I also remember hearing the word 'crazy' when people talked about him. But Sue, to me, Doug doesn't look, act, or seem to be crazy. He's been nothing but nice and normal to me." With that, Sue began refreshing my memories:

- Doug had not lived a happy family life in any sense of the word. His father was hot-tempered and extremely abusive to everyone, especially toward Doug. His father was so angry and abusive toward Doug that one day, as his anger grew, he took an ax and slammed it into Doug's head. Doug was only nine years old.

- His mom rushed him to the hospital. Hours later, the surgeon advised they had done their best. However, the injury caused severe brain damage. The doctor informed her of the possible treatments and medications that would help him live as normal a life as possible. They could not afford additional surgeries or special treatments. Therefore, the medications that were to be taken for the remainder of his life were immediately prescribed.

I had no recollection of being told the following:

- Through the years, he was expelled from multiple schools for improper behavior and fighting.
- As a young adult, he was incarcerated numerous times for violent disorderly conduct and being the instigator of or involved in bar brawls.

- Years later, after securing a job, settling down, marrying the love of his life, and starting a family, he viciously accused his wife and his best friend of having an affair. He violently attacked and seriously injured his friend and almost killed his wife. Charges were filed. He was found guilty of attempted murder and immediately incarcerated. This was the prison term he had recently completed and from which he had been released.

I was stunned. This couldn't be the same guy. He was so nice. He didn't seem to have an angry or "crazy" bone in his body. I expressed these thoughts to Sue, and she replied, "Yes, I'm thanking God, he's been taking his meds regularly. They help him greatly. So, let's pray he keeps taking them. He is a different man while on them. Now, let's head for bed and pray for the best Thanksgiving ever!"

Almost everyone got up early the next morning. Final preparations for the Thanksgiving Day get-together were in full swing. The aromas of Thanksgiving dinner and the joys of family filled the house as everyone arrived with their favorite dishes. It was great seeing everyone and getting updates on what was happening in their lives.

We agreed it had been a wonderful day for all as everyone left with full tummies and a to-go container in hand. However, I found one thing to be strange. Doug had been missing for most of the day. When he was there, he'd briefly smile at me, get some food, stay for a couple of minutes, and without saying much to anybody, go back to the camper with food in hand. The last time he left, he never returned until the next morning. What was up with that?

As the last family members left, Sue and I started cleaning up the messes the day had left behind and reminiscing about the events of the day. It was past midnight when I flopped on the couch, declaring we were done. Sue went to bed soon thereafter. We were extremely tired but glad we could sleep in. Upon awakening, we wouldn't be facing the chore we'd just completed. Thoughts drifted through my mind of what my last day with them might hold as I fell into a deep sleep.

Have you ever slept so deeply and soundly that when you woke up, you couldn't immediately remember where you were? That's what happened to me as a strange male voice startled me awake, asking, "Are you going to sleep all day?"

It had been years since a man's voice woke me up in the morning! My groggy mind couldn't identify the voice. Where was I, and what was a man doing in my room? As my eyes opened and the confused grogginess dissipated, the reality of where I was became clear. Sue was in the kitchen making a pot of coffee. Doug, who had asked the question, was looking down at me, saying he was sorry for startling me. Everyone got a chuckle out of it once I explained my confusion. I felt like a fool.

Sue and I spent most of the day reminiscing and catching up with what was happening in our lives. However, my focus quickly shifted when Doug rudely interrupted, asking whether I was ignoring him and whether I intended to spend the whole day with Sue. I immediately decided that the latter part of my day would be spent with him. We got to know each other better as we talked and walked down the two-mile, tree-lined path to the highway.

He guardedly shared things about his life as we walked. In his mind, the hard life he had led was not his fault. He put all the blame on his father and other family members. He also explained that this was why he had excluded himself from the family's Thanksgiving festivities. He was trying to start a new life. However, his family wasn't giving him a chance because they had all branded him based on his past. It was the only thing they ever talked about. He didn't want to talk to them or allow them the opportunity to ask questions. He knew where those conversations would lead.

Doug ended the conversation by saying, "Nancy, it seems like everyone is trying to put me back into the prison of my past. I don't think I'm that person anymore. Nor do I think I belong in that prison. I want to start a new life. That's all I want." My heart ached. I certainly identified with the desire to start a new life. I felt sorry for him.

That night, we cuddled on the couch and watched TV after dinner. It felt good to be held in his arms and have his gentle kisses placed on my temple. I hadn't gotten that type of attention in years and was loving it. Later that evening, he invited me to spend my last night with him. My brain shouted "No", but my mouth said "Yes." And together we left for the camper.

Once we settled into bed, he reiterated his desire to start anew and added that he wanted to do it with me. I was stunned as he continued saying, "I want to go to Ohio with you tomorrow and start my new life with you because I love you."

Not believing what he had said, I exclaimed, "Doug, we just met! We don't even know each other that well. There's no way you could be in love with me in such a short time."

He angrily bolted out of bed, hysterically yelling all kinds of vulgar things about me, and started throwing anything he could get his hands on at me. His facial features became distorted as his angry tirade grew. His rage was fierce and lasted what seemed like forever. His rant ended as he stood above me and shouted, "Yes, I do love you, and you can and will learn to love me too, if you take me back to Ohio with you."

Fear pierced through my body as my brain quietly cried and questioned, "What's going on? Who is this man yelling and throwing things at me?" He is definitely not the man I've known for the past couple of days. He doesn't even look or sound like him. Could he actually be crazy? How could I have been so blind and stupid? Why didn't I listen to Sue? What have I done? What am I going to do? Lord, help me!

His rant finally ended by telling me he'd sleep on the floor, and we'd talk about it in the morning. Too scared to say a word, I curled up in the corner of the bed and slept fitfully through the night.

I quietly woke up and quickly exited the camper early the next morning. Doug was still half asleep on the floor as he asked me where I was going. My reply was, "I'm headed for the house."

Sue offered me a cup of coffee as I entered and said, "Darlin', you look like death warmed over. Didn't you sleep at all last night?' After telling her what had transpired the night before, she hugged me, saying, "Girl, I tried to warn you, but you wouldn't listen. Nevertheless, I'm here for you now. When he comes in, I'll stand by you and support your efforts in telling him he will not be going back to Ohio with you.

Minutes later, Doug walked in with a packed duffel bag hanging over his shoulder and announced, "I'm ready to go!"

Sue immediately interjected, "What are you talking about? You're not going anywhere." An argument broke out between them as she attempted to detail the reasons why he couldn't and wouldn't be leaving with me. They ranged from his mandatory appointments with his probation officer to the fact that we hardly knew each other.

Doug's fists clenched harder with every word she spoke. Being fearful that he might slug her, I stepped between them and yelled, "Stop it!" And amazingly, they did.

Gently taking Doug's arm, prayers were shot up to the Lord asking Him to give me the words to say that would get me back to Ohio safely and soundly without him.

The Lord came through as I said, "Doug, Sue is right. You have responsibilities here that you must attend to. You want to start a new life, and that's understandable. However, the type of relationship you desire with me takes time. Building a relationship with anybody always takes time. We hardly know each other. I don't know if I even want the type of relationship you desire with me. Getting to know each other will be essential to determine that. You can't go with me now. Time is needed to find out if the relationship you want with me is even possible."

With goodbyes shared with Sue and Ben, I was ready to head for Ohio. Doug was outside waiting to walk me to the car. We hugged, but the kiss he wanted to give me was denied. I gave him my address and said he could write to me if he wanted. I hopped into my car and said, "Goodbye."

I thanked God for being safely homeward bound as I drove down the dirt road to the highway. Gratitude was also expressed to Him for helping me dodge the "Doug bullet" and for making me smart enough not to give him my phone number. There was no way I wanted to talk to him. He scared me half to death.

The long drive home offered me plenty of time to consider what had transpired over the past days between Doug and me. But, more specifically, why did they happen?

The crushing "ah-ha" moment came when I realized everything that had occurred was caused by the choices I had made and the thoughts I chose to think. Devastation filled me. I had not wanted to, and therefore failed, to take my thoughts captive to make them obedient to God. I had brought it all upon myself. The remaining hours of the trip home were spent asking God to forgive me, help me never to fail to take captive my thoughts again, and help me renew my mind to make my thoughts more like His. These prayers continued throughout the night until I fell asleep safe and sound in my own bed back in Ohio.

The next morning, as I got ready for church, I told the Lord that the battle to renew my mind to His ways had been rekindled. From the depths of my heart, I committed to focus my mind on His ways and not the world's. We were going to win this battle together.

> ***Words of Wisdom:*** *The mind is a powerful thing God has created within us. It is where our thoughts begin, and they impact all we say and do. The devil knows it, too. Our minds are Satan's playground. He's an expert player in them and knows how to use our thoughts against us. Even the great Apostle Paul said in Romans 7:22–25 (NLT), "I love God's law with all my heart. But there is another power within me that is at war with my mind. This power makes me a slave to the sin that is still within me. Oh, what a miserable person I am! Who will free me from this life that is dominated by sin and death? Thank God! The answer is in Jesus Christ our Lord. So you see how it is: In my mind I really want to obey God's law, but because of my sinful nature I am a slave to sin." However, Paul knew God was his strength in the fight and was assured that even though the righteous fall seven times, they will rise again (Proverbs 24:16).*
>
> *Like Paul, we must fight this battle against the devil and take captive every one of our thoughts to make them obedient to God. If we don't, I guarantee the devil will fill them with lies*

that blind us to the truth. The devil loves to put our focus on the ways of the world and away from God's truths.

The battleground is within your mind. Focus on God and His truths. Daily, spend time with God and get into His Word. Trust Him in all things. Steadfastly fight the battle with God by your side. And remember the following Scriptures:

- ***Romans 12:2*** *Don't copy the behavior and customs of this world, but let God transform you into a new person by changing the way you think. Then you will learn to know God's will for you, which is good and pleasing and perfect (NLT).*
- ***Proverbs 4:23*** *Be careful how you think; your life is shaped by your thoughts (GNT).*
- ***Ephesians 4:23–24*** *Let the Spirit change your way of thinking and make you into a new person. You were created to be like God" (CEV).*
- ***Romans 8:6*** *The mind governed by the flesh is death, but the mind governed by the Spirit is life and peace.*

It felt so good to be safely back in Ohio. A strong desire to forget all about Doug filled me. I didn't want to think or even talk about him. With those thoughts in mind, I decided to tell no one, even my twin sister, about him. He was in my shameful past, and that's where he was going to stay.

~ 3 ~
READY, SET, GO!

All items on my to-do list were completed by Thanksgiving Day. My entire family, except for my daughter who lived in Arkansas, gathered to celebrate the day. Our time together was filled with love, and the Thanksgiving dinner spread was fabulous. We all had much to be thankful for. It proved to be a blessed day of thanksgiving to God.

However, it was now the Monday after Thanksgiving and the day I had been waiting for. It was the first day of my purpose-filled job with the Central Ohio Small Business Development Center (COSBDC).

Excitement and a hint of nervous anticipation ran through me as I got ready for work. A new series of firsts was about to begin. I was about to become the first special programs coordinator for the COSBDC. It would also be the first time in years that I would not be "The Boss." Now, that was truly something to be thankful for.

As I drove to my new beginning, my thoughts wandered back to three months earlier. I was driving around Dallas, crying, pounding my steering wheel, and screaming, "Lord! I hate what I'm doing. It's just a job! Lord, I don't want 'just a job' and I especially don't want the one I'm in! I no longer want to be an upwardly mobile Exec! All

I want to do is what I love doing. I want a purpose-driven position in which I can use every talent, skill, and ability you've blessed me with in achieving its purpose."

It was then that I heard, *Well, honey, what do you want?* I immediately responded that I wanted a position similar to the one I had with the Indiana Small Business Development Center. However, this time I didn't want to be the "executive director" of anything. I wanted to help people start and grow their businesses, conduct and coordinate seminars and special events, focus my energies on developing women-owned businesses, and strengthen the involvement of community professionals in supporting them all. My plea ended with, "Lord, all I want to do is use the talents, skills, and abilities You've blessed me with as I serve You, serving others. That's what I want to do." To which He quietly responded, *Okay. I'll see what I can do.*

That memory was followed by what happened the following week. I woke up praying, "Lord, I've asked You to open doors to job opportunities. I have this overwhelming feeling that today is the day You'll open those doors for me. Show me 'wherever' my home and new position will be." And with that, I began the search and prayed, "Lord, if the opportunity lies within all these newspapers or all the online searches I'm going to do, let it shout my name!"

Hours later, absolutely nothing had shouted my name. Feeling discouraged and defeated, I frustratingly said, "Lord, I don't understand. I thought this was the day."

Instantly, the gentle voice of God spoke to me and said, *But, honey, you haven't searched one key state in your online search.* I sat up straight and said, "Oh, Lord, not Ohio! You know I seriously dislike winter weather and said I'd never move back there." However, after wrestling with that thought, I finally said, "Okay, I'll do it just to make You happy."

Going back online, I keyed in the Columbus Dispatch and entered four keywords into their classified job postings. Every keyword had matches, but only one keyword, *marketing*, had one post. I chose to click on the single match.

The post popped up on the screen. Its header stated, "Better Job, Better Place to Live." I chuckled and thought, "Oh, Lord, you do have a sense of humor, don't You?" And I heard His quiet reply, *Well, that's what you want, isn't it?*

The post read: The Greater Columbus Chamber of Commerce is in search of a business advisor and analyst for its Central Ohio Small Business Development Center (COSBDC). Oh my gosh! It was the same National Small Business Development program I had worked for in Indiana!

Tears instantly streamed down my face as I put the palm of my hand on the computer screen, saying, "Oh! My! Gosh! Lord, this is Your answer. This is the day! And it's exactly what I asked You to provide!"

Long story short, two weeks later, I entered the COSBDC executive director's office, and the interview began. It went extremely well, even when she leaned forward and said, "Nancy, I must make quite a direct statement now." I knew what she was going to say. It was the most worrying concern I had throughout the entire interview process. I began praying, "Lord, give me the words." My worries were confirmed as she leaned forward, gently shaking my resume, and said, "One would think that if my position were open, my position would be the one you truly want."

The words that came out of my mouth were definitely from God. I leaned toward her and whispered, "One would assume that, would they not?" I sat up straight, pointed across her desk, and said, "No, if they thought that, they would be dead wrong. Been there! Done that! I know what you're going through as director of a regional center. There is no way I want to be 'the boss' anymore. All I want to do is what I absolutely loved doing in that position without all the executive director hassles and headaches."

We laughed as we both knew what I was talking about. She continued by confirming that I was interviewing for the business analyst position but added that she was also interviewing candidates to fill a newly created position within the Center. She then asked if I would be interested in hearing more about this new position. Without hesitation, I said, "Yes."

The position had taken her a year to create and propose to her Board. The final sign-off signatures to initiate the search and hiring process had been secured two weeks prior to my interview with her. That's when my brain began shouting, "Oh, my gosh, Lord, I've lived in Texas for almost a year and responded to their post two weeks ago. I don't know what's going on here, Lord, but Your hand is in this."

The title given to the new position was "special programs coordinator." The person would work closely with the director to create and establish new programs, as well as strengthen existing programs and services offered by the Center. The job description blew me away! It was like it had been tailor-made for me!

My visible outward demeanor was calm and attentive as she shared the position's responsibilities. But what was happening inside of me was anything but calm and attentive. I sat quietly nodding my head. However, my inner being was joyously jumping around like an excited little girl and shouting, "Oh, my gosh, Lord! She is detailing everything I asked you for only weeks ago as I drove around Dallas. Oh, my gosh, Lord! Your hands are all over this. You are answering my plea and pouring it into my lap."

The director gave me the choice of which of the two opportunities I would truthfully want. I replied, "You don't even need to ask. My heart's desire is to do exactly what you have just described."

Her response made my day as she said, "Great! I knew as soon as I read your resume that you were the one. You've got the job! However, I need several weeks to get my Board's final sign-off approval before making it official. Expect a call in about two to three weeks. Her call came, and I was now happily in Ohio, getting ready to experience my first day as the COSBDC's first special programs coordinator.

As I walked through the main entrance to the Chamber of Commerce's offices, God ignited a sense of excitement and enthusiasm within me. I remember thinking, *God, I wonder if this is how Your people felt when You sparked the sense of excitement and enthusiasm within them as they began building Your temple. If so, I want to tell You that's exactly what is pulsating through every inch of me right now!*

I was excited about starting the job God had created for me. I was ready to utilize every skill and ability He had blessed me with to build it strong. My overwhelming feeling of enthusiasm was grounded in the realization of who my God was and what He had done to bring me to this point in my life. And as I entered the Chamber's main entrance, I knew a purposeful career awaited me.

The COSBDC offices were on the fourth floor. Linda, who was the Center's director and now my new boss, warmly greeted me as she exited the elevator. As the elevator took us up to the Center's offices, she explained that the fourth floor was also known as the economic development floor. It was where all efforts to make it happen happened.

A tour of the offices and introductions to staff members were given. As we walked toward her office, she pointed to a cluster of four work cubicles and said, "The front cubicle is your new home away from home, but we'll get to that by the end of the day." In the past, I'd always had my own private office. The thought of not having one hadn't even crossed my mind.

We got down to business the minute we entered her private office. The entire day was spent reviewing the strengths and weaknesses of the Center's four existing programs and services.

As Linda concluded her extensive review, she looked at me and said, "Nancy, I hope you now fully understand that I meant it when I said I knew you were the one for the job." Pointing at the tons of program files we had covered, she added, "There ya go! They're all yours. Build them. Make them better and stronger. Your background shows you can."

Linda helped me lug all the files out to my desk. With that task completed, she reintroduced me to Janet, the Center's administrative assistant, gestured toward the large file cabinets designated as mine, and told us both to "Get them all organized and filed away." As Linda headed back to her office, she looked over her shoulder and once again said, "They're all yours, Nancy. Build them strong and make 'em work. Let's get the job done."

My first mental reaction to what had just happened was, *Wow. Linda is the prime example of the driver leadership style!* I bet her picture is posted above its definition, with the subtitle "Just Get It Done" underneath.

However, her final comment brought back memories from years ago. It was when I began serving as the executive director of the East Central Indians' Small Business Development Center. That Chamber's leadership had said the very same thing to me on my first day. That memory reignited my focus and energy. I was more than ready to utilize every skill and ability God had blessed me with to build the Center's programs, make them strong, and make them work.

Jo called that night and invited me over for dinner. My favorite self-invented song has always been "I Didn't Have to Cook," so I immediately accepted her invitation. She thought it would be a prime opportunity to get a play-by-play update on how my first day went. I looked forward to sharing the events of the day with her.

When I arrived, not only was dinner awaiting me, but also some mail that I had received from my former employer, the Texas State Chamber of Commerce. It was my last severance paycheck, along with a letter explaining that my healthcare insurance would continue through the end of the year. My first thought was, *Oh, that's nice.* However, I abruptly stopped, looked at Jo, and excitedly asked, "Oh my gosh! Jo, do you know what this means?"

Here's what it meant. On my first day working for the COSBDC, I received my last check from my former employer. I had always gotten paid every two weeks, and I'd get my first paycheck from the COSBDC in two weeks! Plus, the health insurance offered through the COSBDC would go into effect the very next day after the Texas Chamber's coverage would be terminated.

With that explained, pure joy filled us both as I exclaimed, "God is so good! He's taking care of me. He's got me covered. And praise God, He hasn't missed a beat in doing it!"

The evening spent with Jo and Ken was filled with sharing updates of the day and rejoicing over what God was doing in my life and within theirs.

> ***Words of Wisdom:*** *Don't take anything that happens in your life for granted. There is no such thing as a coincidence when it comes to God and His plan for you! There is always a purpose behind everything He does. Wake up! Be aware of how He is working within your life. And then, rejoice in Him! All you must do is get out of His way and do what He would have you do. Trust in God, no matter what! Yes, it may be difficult at first, but the more you do it, the easier it becomes because He'll show up and give you cause to celebrate!*

That night, as I went to bed back at home, I thanked God for how He had and was still taking care of me. I remember thinking, *Lord, tomorrow morning I am going to do exactly what you told Gideon to do in the Book of Judges. I'm going to go to the office and 'Go in the strengths I have.' Lord, I'm also looking forward to seeing how You use those strengths, make them even stronger, and see what You will accomplish through them.*

I was relishing a spiritual high with and in God. Given the miracles the Lord had done in my life over the past four months and the fact that I was surrounded only by loving, Christ-centered people during that time, I was blessed and rejoicing in my private world with Him.

However, as I reentered and dove back into the "real world," several former traits within me began to resurface. I would soon learn how truly difficult it is to maintain "a renewed mind." And believe me, not maintaining a renewed mindset in Christ only leads to internal and external troubles.

~ 4 ~
TAKING CARE OF BUSINESS

A wholehearted desire to serve the Center penetrated through me as the second day on the job began. I was ready to take care of business and use every talent and skill I had.

The day started with a special SBDC full staff meeting. The Chamber's vice president of economic development welcomed me aboard and reintroduced me to Martin, the director of the Chamber's Small Business Council (SBC). Martin and I would soon develop a great working relationship that would last for years.

Three other COSBDC staff advisors were introduced. All of them were men. Mark had gotten the advisory position for which I had originally applied and was now the gentleman who occupied the cubicle directly behind mine. The other two advisors, Josh and Matt, were seldom in the office, as they worked in and served the other counties within our regional service area. Later, I learned that all three of them were wonderful believers in Christ. And as time passed, this would become a blessing.

Linda had asked me to meet with her directly after the meeting, and it started immediately as I walked into her office. She reiterated her strong desire for me to focus my energies and time on strengthening the programs and services we had covered the day before. However, there was a hitch to it all. A little more than 25 percent of my time had to be spent providing one-on-one business counseling to start-up and existing business owners.

Why? The Center's major funding was provided through a federal grant program administered by the Small Business Administration (SBA). This grant provided 50 percent of the Center's needed funds. At that time, all SBA funding under this grant program was only driven by the one-on-one counseling hours provided through the Center. Therefore, a little less than 75 percent of my time could be spent on revamping, strengthening, and promoting the following three major programs and services:

1. THE EXPERT'S VOLUNTEER OPPORTUNITY—At the time, this program only campaigned for community business professionals to voluntarily serve as advisors to the Center's clients.
2. THE WNET PROGRAM (The Women's Network for Educational Training)—As a former SBDC Director in Indiana, I knew it was an antiquated SBA mentoring program that paired an existing woman business owner to serve as a volunteer mentor to an entrepreneurial-minded woman wanting to start her own business. Given my experience with WNET, I knew it wouldn't work. But Linda still wanted me to "give WNET my best shot and promote it as it was."

3. THE CENTER'S SMALL BUSINESS WORKSHOPS AND SPECIAL EVENTS—Both were few and far between due to the lack of manpower, limited budget, and bandwidth to support them.

A silent prayer of thanks for the opportunity to apply my program development experience was lifted to God as I left our meeting. I knew that changes could be made somehow.

However, over time, creating new beneficial programs while revamping and strengthening existing programs would not prove to be quick and easy for the following reasons:

- Each existing program had its daunting problems.
- The Ohio SBDC State Lead Center had a mandate that all OSBDC business advisors be "certified" to prove their capability to serve. My out-of-state SBDC certifications were not recognized, and "testing out" was not an option. I had to take the OSBDC certification course. It was a three-month, fast-paced college-level course. Requirements included class time, essay submissions, and final tests on every business topic. The course was offered six months after I started, and three months later, I passed it with flying colors, receiving my OSBDC Certification.
- The last reason was most daunting and difficult to deal with and overcome. It was the growing and negative opinion and

attitude I held toward my boss. She angered and frustrated me by questioning almost everything I did. Her actions and attitudes made me think she didn't believe that I truly did not want her job. It seemed as though she was attempting to sabotage everything I did or wanted to do. And at times, I thought she was downright rude, condescending, and inconsiderate to everyone. I knew she desired to be a leader and build a team, but everything she was doing was tearing it apart.

There were many nights that I cried, "Lord, why does she act that way and treat me like she does? All I'm doing is the job she wants me to do, and I think I'm doing it well. Lord, I am beginning to despise her. You know, I seriously dislike feeling that way about anybody. Please help me. I want to be a good team player and help her build the program in which we both work."

One day, as Mark and I were having a private conversation, I shared some of my observations and feelings about Linda. He empathized with me. He had, at times, seen and felt the same. But instead of feeding my anger, he looked at me and said, "Nancy, you've painted a pretty clear picture of what an enemy looks like. However, instead of hating her, which only makes the situation worse, why not do what the Bible tells us to do? You know it tells us to love our enemies and pray for them. That's what I've been doing for some time now, and it's helped. Try it. Pray for her and see if love and understanding, instead of hate, grow within you."

His response floored me because, at that moment, I felt anything but love toward her. All afternoon, I pondered his recommendation and finally realized he was right. That night, prayers for her were lifted to the Lord. And as I did, I also asked God to forgive me for having previously prayed only for myself and the situations around me.

Granted, the first couple of times I prayed for her were tough. But the more I did, the easier it got. Mark and I even started praying for her while at work. The results of our prayers slowly began to manifest, and a compassionate spirit began to grow in me. Oh, she and I still had our days and moments. However, they were easier to handle, for when they did happen, Mark and I would look at each other, smile, and begin to silently pray.

Success in revamping the Center's Community Volunteer program came together quickly due to a similar program I had created for the Indiana SBDC. The new program would be known as "The Professional Resource Opportunity Service" (PROS Program). It would significantly enhance the business advisory services provided to the Center's clients, increase the benefits offered to professional volunteers, and strengthen the Center'scapacity to deliver high-quality seminars and special events. It was a "Win-Win" for everyone involved.

The grand launch day for the PROS Program finally arrived. A handful of community leaders and business experts had been invited to the unveiling and kick-off. I was thrilled and took great pride in all I had accomplished and created. I couldn't wait for the unveiling to begin. However, as you read on, keep in mind that Proverbs 16:18 reminds us that pride comes before the fall.

Linda stood at the head of the table, looked at the community and business leaders seated around the table, and said, "You've been invited here to be the first to hear about and hopefully become involved in a new program that I have been working on for the past months."

With that, my mind screamed, *What! You haven't done diddly-squat. I've done all the work. I was the one who created this for the Center!* A split second later, my disgusted, uncontrolled thought came flying out of my mouth, "What!? No, you have not!"

Smiles around the table immediately disappeared, and the room fell silent. I was devastatingly embarrassed. I couldn't believe my thoughts had flown out of my mouth, so I began praying, "Oh Lord, forgive me and help me." *I thought I had demolished that prideful 'I, Me, My, Mine, I Can Do All Things Through Me, Myself, and I' attitude. But apparently, it's still inside me.*

Linda took a deep breath, calmly looked at me and those seated around the table, and said, "Well, Nancy's right. We, together, have been working on it for months, and we're extremely excited to share it with you now."

The meeting proceeded as we shared the program's details and benefits. All were encouragingly enthused and interested in becoming actively involved. Many took the information back to their offices to share it with their staff. The day ended without either Linda or me speaking to each other. I left work feeling ashamed of what I had done and of the awkward position my outburst had put her in.

Words of Wisdom: *Remember, God loves us even though we sin. However, in His Word, He has given us many recommendations to follow to help us fight our battle against sin. Here are a few. Remember them. You'll need them:*

- *2 Corinthians 10:5b "Take captive every thought to make it obedient to Christ."*
- *Matthew 15:18 "The things that come out of a person's mouth come from the heart, and these defile them."*
- *Psalm 21:23 (NLT) "Watch your tongue and keep your mouth shut, and you will stay out of trouble."*

- *Proverbs 13:3 (NLT) "Those who control their tongue will have a long life; opening your mouth can ruin everything."*
- *James 1:19–20 "Everyone should be quick to listen, slow to speak and slow to become angry because human anger does not produce the righteousness that God desires."*

That night, I felt like a shameful fool and just wanted to lie there and die. My spirit was ripped apart by what I had said. I was sorry for it and frustrated with myself. Refocusing my thoughts, I asked the Lord to help me understand why Linda was always getting on my last nerve.

As I pondered that question, I heard a quiet voice inside my thoughts say, *Nancy, it's because her driven leadership style reminds you of an earlier you.* I was thunderstruck! It was true! It did, and it was! Her leadership style was reminiscent of exactly what I had held over two decades ago when I started in the business world. I had been extremely career-minded and goal-oriented. Everyone knew I desired to move up in the world. I needed to always be "in command, in control," and take full credit for all accomplishments realized. Oh my gosh, it was true. Linda reminded me of the "used to be" me!

With this realization, I thanked God for patiently and lovingly teaching me that holding this mindset only brought defeat and ruin to all I thought, wanted, and desired. I had learned the hard way, and I didn't want that to happen to Linda.

Immediately, my prayers focused on asking God how I could best address what had happened during the meeting. I needed to confess that my outburst was wrong and ask for her forgiveness. I wanted to confirm that she was my boss and that I in no way desired her responsibilities. My true desire was to be a good team player and, in time, respectfully serve as a caring mentor, sharing helpful insights to strengthen her leadership and team-building efforts.

Several days later, I visited her office to inform her of my agenda for the following day. I stood there momentarily waiting for her reply. She did not respond nor look at me as I did. So, I said, "Okay, see you tomorrow." But as I headed for the elevator, I abruptly stopped as God's quiet voice within me said, *Nancy, you just spoke to her as though you were her boss. You are not. Go back. Tell her you're sorry and ask her out to lunch. I'm opening a door for you to make things right.* Immediately, I returned to her open office door and said, "Linda, I am so sorry. I just talked to you like I used to as boss over my staff. Please forgive me. You're my boss. I guess old habits are hard to stop."

With that, she turned, chuckled, and said, "Nancy, it's okay. I knew you meant no disrespect. However, you're right, old habits do tend to be difficult to change." A brief conversation followed, and she accepted my invitation to lunch later in the week.

Walking to my car, I said, "Okay, Lord, I'm trusting You in this. You've opened the door, now please give me the words to say during our lunch together.

The luncheon proved to be one orchestrated by God. Linda dove right into business. We discussed progress on securing a contract with a leading Florida theme park to provide their day-long multimedia professional development program, the revitalization of the WNET program, and the outstanding response to the PROS program.

God then opened the door and gave me the words to admit what I had done was wrong, tell her I was sorry, and humbly ask her forgiveness for my terrible outburst. I sincerely confirmed that she was the boss, and I shared several reasons why I no longer wanted the responsibilities of being one.

To say it was a great luncheon meeting would be an understatement. We both left feeling that the comradeship we had felt during my job interview had been restored. Over time, team-building insights were shared and integrated into her leadership style, and our camaraderie grew stronger throughout her tenure as director and my boss.

The Center's capacity to offer seminars and professional development programs also increased as teamwork attitudes grew among the Center, the Small Business Council, the Chamber of Commerce, and its volunteer base.

A great example of this was the joint effort that brought the Florida theme park's day-long professional development program to Columbus in mid-September of 2000. The registration fee to attend was extremely high due to pricing mandates set by the theme park company. I thought very few would pay the high-dollar registration fee. However, the response was overwhelming. It was sold out and went off without a hitch thanks to everyone involved.

Words of Wisdom: *We all cope with difficult people who irritate, anger, madden, and frustrate us. And no matter the type of personal or working relationships we're in, remember, no one is perfect at dealing with them. The challenge in improving how we deal with them lies in our response. The secret to meeting this challenge is to take control of the emotions we show, the words we speak, and the actions we purposefully take.*

The Word of God tells us in Ephesians 4:31–32 to "Get rid of all bitterness, rage and anger, brawling and slander, along with every form of malice. Be kind and compassionate to one another, forgiving each other, just as in Christ God forgave you." In Titus, the Word continues to share that we should be ready to do whatever is good, not insult anyone, be nonviolent, considerate, and always be gentle in word and deed toward everyone.

Follow these tips shared by Pastor Rick Warren during one of his Daily Hope podcasts. They are worthy of being remembered and practiced because they are spot-on and effective. Realign your thought process and:

- *Listen to what they have to say with an open mind and caring spirit.*
- *Think before you respond in actions or words.*
- *Before you say a word, think of this Scripture verse: "Lord, help me control my tongue; help me be careful about what I say" (Psalm 141:3, NCV).*
- *Be gentle in your tone and tactfully truthful in your responses. Tact and tone should always go together. Remember what Proverbs 15:1 (GNT) says, "A gentle answer quiets anger, but a harsh one stirs it up." (It isn't what you say, it's how you say it.)*

- *Remember, you are never persuasive when you're abrasive.*
- *Rudeness ruins relationships of any kind.*
- *Nagging is never right, nor does it work.*
- *Think of it this way: if you want to respond the way Jesus would, show them compassion in your words and deeds.*

The first full year serving as the special programs coordinator for the Center proved to be remarkably productive and beneficial to both the Center and the business community. However, it was most miraculously beneficial to and for me personally.

To explain what made that first year truly most miraculously beneficial to and for me, I must take you back in time into my personal life. Come with me now as I take you back to my first day working for the OSBDC and into 2000.

As I share what was happening in my personal life, please remember that both my personal and professional lives were moving in sync throughout it all. I think you'll agree with me and find it to be miraculous as well. And believe it or not, I'm praising and thanking God for it all!

~

My first day on the job was personally delightful. I immediately felt welcomed and a member of the team. Many co-workers brought Thanksgiving leftovers to share over lunch. It was great and everyone laughed as I entered the breakroom singing my favorite song about not having to cook.

We were also celebrating the fact that the month to come would be delightfully easy. Demand for business assistance in December would be almost nonexistent. It was the perfect time to finalize plans for the upcoming year and address internal operational needs.

The Center set a prime example of this, ushering in December by hiring a new OSBDC administrative assistant. Her name was Rose, and she proved herself to be amazing in more than one way. She was not only extremely competent in her computer, office, and organizational skills, but her faith and trust in God were both strong. She didn't hesitate to proclaim it either. Rose sat to my right, and Mark sat behind me in our cubicle area. It was as though I was surrounded by the Lord at work with me. We would soon serve as each other's Christ-centered "iron sharpens iron" support base. I couldn't have asked for anything better.

There was another change in the Chamber's operations during December. The Chamber had experienced increasing security issues. Multiple and unknown individuals had entered the building and gained access to the second through fourth-floor offices.

Therefore, a security swipe card system was installed within the building's exterior doors and elevator system. After it was installed, no one could get into the building or use the elevators without a swipe card. Every client or meeting attendee had to gain approved access into the building and be escorted to their designated meeting room on any floor. I found dealing with this change to be a terrible pain in my posterior. However, as you read on, please keep in mind God's timing is perfect.

Personally, December proved to be a productive and joyful month, filled with Christmas parties, church services, and family celebrations. The only thing left was to attend New Year's church services and celebrate the new millennium with my family. That is, until my home doorbell rang the night before New Year's Eve.

As I turned on the porch light and looked out the window, I couldn't believe who was standing there. *Doug!* I hadn't seen or heard from him since our Thanksgiving ordeal. Panic pierced through my body as my confused mind screamed, *What is he doing here? How did he get here? Lord, what's going on?*

I opened the door, and without hesitation, Doug pushed me to the side, crossed the threshold of my home, and with a smile on his face and a duffel bag over his shoulder said, "Hi, honey. I'm home!"

Dear Reader: *You are about to enter the most terrifying, violent, problem-oriented, and confusing five months of my life. I know that may seem like a short time, but it felt like a never-ending eternity to me. The sequence of events is blurred and melded in my memory, but the events themselves and the feelings they evoke remain vivid in my mind today. It all happened because of the choices I had made and the thoughts I chose to think during my early Thanksgiving visit to Arkansas. Over these months, God, once again, disciplined and taught me the errors of my ways. Hebrews 12:11 says, "No discipline seems pleasant at the time, but painful." And oh, it was! Hebrews also encourages us to take God's discipline seriously and not give up when He teaches or corrects us because He disciplines those He loves. And in the end, His discipline will produce a harvest of righteousness and peace for those who have been trained by it. And oh yes, it does! I was disciplined hard and trained well during these months. However, I never gave up, and He never gave up on me! He was with me through it all. Come see how God taught me, went before me, and took care of me during this most difficult time. It painfully taught and brought me thousands of steps closer to becoming the "I Believe and Trust in God, No Matter What!" person I wanted to become.*

~ 5 ~
NEW YEAR—DREADFUL REALITIES

My past had reentered my life. Fear filled my heart as "It" stood there looking back at me, dressed in what looked like black biker garb. Terrified thoughts flew through my head. *What did he mean he was home? This was and is not his home, and there is no way I want him in my life.* Regrouping my thoughts, I asked, "How did you get here? Are you here for a visit? Why didn't you call me? His response addressed all the questions that were milling in my mind and flying out of my mouth.

Over the past month, he had developed a plan, got a job close to his home in Arkansas, and saved up all his money to buy a bus ticket to Columbus. He hadn't told anyone in Arkansas about his plan, and no one there knew that the final destination of his plan was my home in Columbus. Ohio. He wasn't here for a visit. According to him, he was home to stay and ready to work on the relationship he wanted with me. He had not called because I had only given him my address. Thanks to that, he knew exactly where to go once he arrived in Columbus.

Having heard all of this, I was kicking myself, thinking, *Nancy, how stupid could you be? You should have given him your phone number, not your address. He is now standing in front of you because of your stupid mistake.*

Frantic fear grew as I tried to explain that he couldn't live with me and that this was not his home. We hardly knew each other. Plus, no one in my family even knew he existed. If he wanted to stay, he would have to find somewhere else to live. He couldn't stay and live with me.

His response to all my reasoning was filled with anger as he said, "Well, I'm staying, and we're going to make this my home. I hope you don't have plans for tomorrow night because we're going to celebrate my homecoming together. We're going to ring in 2001 in the privacy of my new home and celebrate the life we'll have together." He threw his duffel bag and faux leather black jacket over his shoulder and said, "I'm tired and going to bed. Where's our bedroom?"

I pointed up the stairs but didn't join him that night. Overwhelming worry merged with my frantic fear as I fitfully fell asleep on the couch. What was I going to do? How could I tell my family—especially my twin sister—about Doug? What explanation could be given to explain what he was doing here? However, as these thoughts billowed through my brain, a realization became clear. I had brought this raging storm upon myself because of the choices I had made in Arkansas. The storm was here and was now upstairs, sleeping in my bed.

With a heavy heart filled with shame and sorrow, I laid the whole situation before God. I pleaded for His forgiveness, strength, safekeeping, and guidance to get me through the tumultuous storm I had brought upon myself. This prayer would be repeated throughout the coming months as I coped with the reality facing me.

> ***Words of Wisdom:*** *When life's troubled storms are outside and all around you, don't allow them to get inside you or get you down. Go vertical instead! Look up and align yourself with the Lord. Run to Him. Tell Him what you're facing and how you see yourself within the situation. Nothing will surprise Him. Yes, He already knows, but He wants to hear it from you. Acknowledge your part in creating the troubled storm. Then ask Him to forgive you. The Word of God tells us that if we ask, we will receive. Ask, He will forgive you, for He is a faithful, loving, and merciful God.*

Two calls were immediately made before Doug woke up the next morning. The first was to my sister to explain that I would not be celebrating New Year's with them, as a friend from Arkansas had unexpectedly come to celebrate it with me. The second call was to Sue.

The surprise and shock of my news were evident in her voice as she said, "So that's where he is!" She continued to explain that, soon after Thanksgiving, Doug had moved back home with his parents. He'd gotten a job, and then two days ago, disappeared without a word to anyone. Everyone was worried, wondering where he could have gone and if he was okay. I assured her that he was okay and told her all about the previous night's events. Her devastated reply was, "Oh, Nancy, I am so sorry."

Mine was, "Yeah, so am I."

Sue gave me his mother's phone number just in case I needed to call her. She also agreed to call his mom and let her know where he was. We both agreed to keep each other posted and to keep the whole situation in our prayers.

The call ended as Doug came downstairs wearing the same black clothes he'd worn the night before and suspiciously asked, "Who were you talking to?" When I told him who, he went into a ranting rage, saying, "Why the heck did you call her? I didn't want anyone to know where I was!" His irate ranting continued as I stood there shocked, thinking, *Lord, help me, and thank You that I didn't tell him Sue was going to call his mom or that I had his mom's phone number.*

The whole ordeal ended with vulgar expletives spewing out of his mouth as he stormed upstairs to take a shower. My nerves felt as though they'd been put into a blender. Yet, I prayed, "Lord, help me! What have I gotten myself into?"

About an hour later, Doug came downstairs. He was wearing an earth-tone shirt and blue jeans. His anger had subsided. He was calm and in a good mood. I was praising God, his mood had changed, and I remember thinking, *Now this is the guy I first met and liked back in Arkansas.*

My fears began to fade as we enjoyed our day talking, sitting together on the couch, munching on snacks, and watching movies on TV. Our still-guarded dinner conversation was good, and with every minute that passed, I became more comfortable around him.

As the night progressed, we turned the television back on to watch the festivities in Times Square. About an hour before the ball dropped, I went out to the kitchen to prepare for our midnight celebration and uncork a bottle of wine. As I did, Doug came out, kissed my temple, and told me he was going to take a quick shower because he wasn't feeling good. I let him hug me, and off he went.

His return downstairs was announced by my cat's crying scream as she flew airborne to the bottom of the stairs. As this happened, I heard Doug heatedly yell, "Dang cat! Get out of my way!" (Wells, he didn't exactly say "dang," but I'm sure you can understand why I edited this.)

I couldn't believe it! He had kicked my cat! I turned, becoming even more concerned as I saw him wearing a black shirt and the black leather pants he had worn earlier. What was going on? What had happened to change his mood? This wasn't "the Doug" who went to take a shower.

His mood and attitude had drastically changed for the worse. Even his facial features, expressions, speech patterns, and mannerisms seemed slightly different for some reason. They were the same as the man who had reentered my life the night before and yelled at me earlier this morning.

The look on his face scared me. The man in black was back, and the fear inside me returned. I remember thinking, *Lord, what the heck is going on!? This isn't the man who, less than an hour ago, went up to take a shower.* My guard was up once again.

We toasted in the New Year as the clock struck midnight. Note that I didn't say "Happy" New Year. I was anything but happy. The ball dropped, and so did my spirit as Doug cruelly grabbed me, encompassed my body with a bear hug that squeezed every ounce of oxygen out of my lungs, and brutally kissed my lips. With vulgar words spewing out of his mouth, he then said, "Come on, woman, we're going to bed and ring in the new year. We're gonna do it all night long." He turned and started to drag me up the stairs. I pleaded with him to stop and tried to fight back to no avail. He kicked the bedroom door open, threw me on the bed, and had his way with me.

Not believing what was happening to me, I cried and prayed, *Lord, help me. This can't be happening to me. This isn't love. This is abuse. There's no love in what he is doing to me, and he intends to do this for hours. Lord, make this stop!*

And that's what God did! After only one sexual encounter, Doug dropped onto the bed, exhausted, and immediately fell asleep. Silently, I cried, thanking God that the brutal ordeal would not last all night. As I drifted off into a fitful sleep, I remember thinking, *Lord, I want no part of this in my life.*

On New Year's morning, so as not to awaken Doug, I quietly went downstairs. When he finally came down, he was wearing his blue jeans and an earth-tone shirt. He seemed a little disturbed, but in a good mood. The day went well, even though his temper briefly flared at times. Everything seemed somewhat back to normal. Yet, all day long, I felt like I was walking on broken glass. His drastic mood swings scared me. Minute by minute, I was apprehensive of what might happen next. That night, I recall thinking it was as if two different people had entered my life.

Going back to work the next day was a blessing. It was so good to get away from it all. I felt safe. My energies and focus were spent on taking care of the business. However, that week initiated the dreaded thoughts of always wondering what mood Doug would be in when I got home from work.

Each night, upon returning home that first week, Doug and I had serious conversations regarding why he couldn't live with me. His rebuttals were always that he loved me, wanted to be in my life, had no money to rent another place, and didn't want to go back to the life he had in Arkansas. These discussions only led to frustrating emotions for both of us. Well, that is, until Doug, wearing his black biker garb, greeted me when I got home from work Friday night.

His heated anger and rage were evident as he announced there would be no further conversations about his not living with me. His brutality mounted as he angrily declared and made it quite clear that he had no intention of leaving. He raised his hand ready to hit me and vulgarly yelled, "I'm staying, and you might as well plan on making me a permanent part of your life." I curled up in a fetal position in my chair. Fearing for my life, I pleaded with him not to hit me, and silently prayed, *Lord, help me please!*

At that very moment, the phone rang. With thanks to God screaming in my head, I quickly got up, ran to answer it, and avoided the physical abuse he was about to inflict upon me.

Oh my gosh! It was Jo calling, wanting to know how my New Year's celebrations went, if my guest was still there, and why I hadn't been over to see her during the past week.

Our conversation was brief, and I knew she could hear Doug constantly asking whom I was talking to. Therefore, vague and guarded answers were given. I told her our New Year was okay. Doug, my guest, was still here and would be staying for a while. My busy work schedule and my guest had prevented me from visiting her. Jo ended the call by saying that she and Ken would love to meet Doug and invited me to bring him over to the house. My shame and fear of being asked any questions about him at that time lead me to fake an enthusiastic reply and I said, "Oh, that would be great. I'll ask him and let you know."

I hung up the phone, and once again, Doug's questions began. "Who were you talking to? Why did they call? What did they want?" "Why did you say it that way?" "Why do they want to meet me?" He didn't trust me, let alone anyone else. After answering them all, I asked if he wanted to meet them. His first response was an adamant and angry "No." However, after explaining how important it would be for him to meet them and how it would help prevent any further concerns from arising on their end, he angrily agreed and stormed upstairs. As he did, I also told him I wasn't feeling well and would be sleeping on the couch that night.

Sleep did not come easily that night. My mind was full of muddled thoughts, and I shared them all with God. I remember asking, "Lord, what have I gotten myself into? I've never experienced such an emotionally cruel relationship like this before in my life. One minute, he says he loves me, and the next minute, he verbally abuses me and acts as though he's ready to beat me. One minute, he says he believes me, but the next, he accuses me and calls me a liar. Lord, his mood swings scare me half to death. It's like I'm living with two different people. Please, Lord, speak to me. Give me some answers." My spirit calmed. I took a deep breath, and as I quietly lay there, a strange, long-ago teenage memory came to mind.

I was watching the movie "The Three Faces of Eve" with my dad. It was released in 1957, won many Academy Awards, and was now released for broadcast on television. My dad said the filmmakers stated it was a true story based on a book about a woman with three different personalities. However, Dad couldn't believe it was true. "Things like that only happen in the movies." He was adamant in believing the filmmakers only promoted it that way to increase ticket sales at the movie theaters. Nonetheless, he had to watch it as it starred one of his favorite actresses, Joanne Woodward.

The movie is about a timid housewife, Eve White, who begins seeing a psychiatrist because of the ongoing severe headaches and inexplicable blackouts she is experiencing. As her sessions progressed, the doctor was stunned when the timid Eve White transformed before his very eyes into a lustful and quite forward woman by the name of Eve Black. Plus, not long after that, a third woman appeared to him. She said her name was Jane. As the story progresses, the doctor diagnoses her as having multiple personalities. The movie concludes as the doctor, through hypnosis and therapy, struggles to help Eve recall the trauma that caused her identity to fracture.

Oh my gosh! Could Doug, given his drastic and devastating life history, be another "Eve"? I then remembered that when the personalities changed, each woman's facial structure and speech patterns changed slightly, and each personality preferred and chose to wear different colors and styles of clothing.

My situation was so similar. However, I told myself it couldn't be true. The movie memory startled me, but I chose to take my dad's side. I slightly chuckled, telling myself not to be stupid and believe that such far-fetched things exist. My dad was right. Those types of things only happen in the movies. I fell asleep that night praying, "Dear God, help me cope and deal with Doug's mood swings and keep me safe from harm."

Words of Wisdom: *When you ask God to speak to you, be still, pay attention, and listen to what He brings into your* *thoughts. You may have reservations and doubts, but be unaware of the true reality of what and why He's brought those thoughts to mind. Open your mind and eyes. Respond to them! Whatever you do, don't disregard them as silly or impossible. He gives them on and with purpose. God knows and understands what you don't. I'd learn this hard lesson within months.*

~ 6 ~
TRYING TO TURN BAD INTO GOOD

Although I didn't want it, Doug was becoming a part of my life's reality. Neither he nor I had the financial wherewithal to find anywhere else for him to live. And I didn't have the financial resources or power to make him go back to where he had come from. He had no money, no car, job, or clothes to speak of. He had no friends, nor did he want a life outside of me and mine. I told myself that my dreaded past mistake was never leaving.

In the face of this unwanted reality, I tried to live my personal life as though nothing had changed. However, with every passing day, so much was changing.

I encouraged him daily to look for a job close to us, explaining that it would not only help cover our increased living expenses but also open up opportunities for him to make some friends of his own. He finally agreed, and at my own expense, two shopping sprees to purchase "job hunting" clothes at a local thrift store followed. Why two sprees?

The first spree resulted in purchasing blue jeans and earth-tone shirts. The second happened immediately after Doug heatedly accused me of buying clothes that he hated. My futile attempts to explain that he had selected them came to no avail. His anger grew with every word I spoke. He threw the clothes at me and angrily ranted that he wouldn't wear them and wanted to burn them. He ended his rant by saying, "I ain't no sissified boy! I'm the man of this house and woman; you better not forget it!"

Accusing aggression and striking fear into any situation was always his ultimate tool to control everything, including me. Therefore, we immediately went to the thrift store. His selections and my purchases that night were two pairs of black jeans and several black shirts and T-shirts.

The visit with Jo and Ken occurred about a week later. It was quite tense and strenuous, and it didn't go well. Within minutes, Doug began pretending to be sick. He didn't interact and hardly spoke a word during the entire visit. His responses to any comment or question were to grimace, make gruntle sounds, or say, "You tell them, honey." My guarded responses prevented me from answering any in-depth questions truthfully because the man in black sat next to me.

The stress-filled visit was short-lived, and I was glad. However, as goodbyes were shared, I prayed they could tell "something" was not right. As we hopped in the car, Doug said, "Well, that went well. But, I'm never going back there, and if you know what's good for you, neither will you." My blood went cold, and fear of what would happen if I did, began to build. And that fear rapidly grew over the following weeks.

After that visit, spending time with both Jo and Ken became almost non-existent. When visits with Jo did happen, they were made on my way home from work and only lasted no more than 15 minutes. Why? Because if I were late or gone too long, according to Doug's timeframe of expectancy, terrible and abusive experiences would await me.

Except for my job and the people I worked with, I was cut off from everything important to me. Contact with my entire family, personal friends, and my church family was forbidden.

He didn't want to go out and do anything together, especially to church. The one time I tried to go by myself, he hid my car keys and didn't return them until later that evening. Church was out of the question. Therefore, having my daily private time with God and reading my Bible became essential. When caught doing either of these things, Doug would brutally accuse me of thinking I was better than him. I denied that accusation every time. However, that didn't stop me. Every day, I secluded myself in either the bathroom or bedroom and spent the time I could with God and in His Word.

Words of Wisdom: *Private time with God is the most important thing you should have if you desire to grow in your walk with Him. Getting together with like-minded believers or being busily involved in a church community are important, as these efforts strongly support your spiritual growth. However, the essential things you need to engage in doing are:*

- *Daily read God's Word and pray.*
- *Memorize verses that speak to you and meditate on them. Hide His Word in your heart!*
- *Absorb it all into your life and live it.*
- *Trust in it. No matter what!*
- *Let the Word of God, the Bible, become your ultimate guide in all you do and say.*

There is no other resource that will guide and strengthen your growth in Him better than His Word. The Bible says in 2 Timothy 3:16–17 (NLT) "All Scripture is inspired by God and is useful to teach us what is true and to make us realize what is wrong in our lives. It corrects us when we are wrong and teaches us to do what is right. [17] God uses it to prepare and equip his people to do every good work."

January bled into February, and no matter how hard I tried, things weren't getting better. They only got worse. Doug had run out of his medications and adamantly refused to go to any doctor or mental health center to get medication or help. Instead, he found alternative illegal drug resources that made everything even worse. His sweeping mood swings drastically increased. His emotional state became seriously unstable. His mounting anger, distrust of anyone, and abuse escalated. The fear of physical harm he created within me was his ultimate tool of control. Therefore, my mandated isolation, his verbal and emotional abuse spewed upon me, and my mounting fear of physical harm were all heightened to the max.

Life with Doug was one of forced seclusion. There were only two times that I was able to convince him to go somewhere with me.

The first was to the local karaoke bar, where I had regularly gone to sing and shoot pool. I'll never forget that night. He was decked out in his black leather biker garb as he came downstairs, announcing he was ready to go. Warning lights went off in my mind. I knew I had to be cautious and be on my best behavior that night. When Doug wore black, it always meant his hateful, bad attitude would be well in play, and trouble would be in the air. I was so right, and our night out was short-lived.

Everyone was thrilled to see me and asked where I'd been and who the man with me was. I saw the smirk on Doug's face as his anger grew. I introduced him to several of the guys I always shot pool with. After the introductions, I turned to order our drinks and, from behind me, heard Doug vehemently ask, "Bastard, who you lookin' at?" The guy didn't even have time to reply before Doug shoved him into the bar and began viciously hitting him with his fist. A fight broke out between the two. Doug was soon and quite reluctantly escorted out of the bar. Embarrassed, crying, and apologizing to everyone, I walked out behind him, never to return to that bar again.

When we got home, Doug accused me of flirting with the guys and even asked how many I had slept with. I told him none, but he refused to believe me. His anger grew as he reached for his pack of cigarettes. I had stopped smoking before moving back to Columbus and didn't allow it in my home. Therefore, even though it was a chilly winter night, I asked him to go outside if he wanted to smoke.

The full force of his verbal wrath broke out on me as he accused me of thinking I was better than him. His vicious, destructive anger grew to a level I had not seen or experienced. He came raging toward me with his clenched fists raised high. Extreme fear of harm and being beaten to death permeated within me as I curled up in a ball and screamed, "Please don't hit me. I'm no better than you. Give me a darn cigarette. I'll smoke it!"

He immediately calmed down, devilishly smiled at me, gave me a cigarette, and lit it for me. We both smoked our cigarettes to its butt. As he finished his cigarette, he bent down, kissed my temple, told me he loved me, and went up to bed.

I slept on the couch that night, my mind filled with troubled thoughts. Oh my gosh, I was taking up the habit of smoking again to save my life from harm. Who was this man living with me? How could he change from foe to friend or vice versa in a split second? I couldn't believe what had just happened.

I truthfully felt like King David must have felt in Psalm 109:3–5 when he said, "With words of hatred they surround me; they attack me without cause. In return for my friendship, they accuse me. They repay me evil for good and hatred for my friendship."

The second time he agreed to go somewhere with me was to a nearby park. It was one of those sunny, unseasonably warm late-winter days. It was a beautiful day and the perfect opportunity to take a walk. Doug agreed but told me he would have to change his clothes before we did and went upstairs to do so. Not more than twenty minutes later, he returned fully dressed in black. The Man in Black stood there with all his biker attitude, telling me he was ready to go.

Having learned my lesson from the past local karaoke bar episode, I automatically began praying, *Oh Lord, help me.* Immediately standing to my feet, I pointed directly at him and heatedly yelled, "I'm not going anywhere with you! I mean it. You might as well go back upstairs and change your clothes into what you had on. I'm not going anywhere with you, and that's final!" He started to rebut, but I held my hand, told him not to say a word, and to get back upstairs. And surprisingly, he did. Doug returned downstairs over an hour later, wearing the clothes he had on earlier in the day.

My private home life would only get worse. Well, that is, except for my nightly private prayer time. That became stronger and more often than at bedtime. Many times over the following days, I'd tell God that I knew He was trying to teach me something extremely important through this difficult time. I'd ask Him to lead, guide, and direct me as He loved and protected me throughout it all. I would also tell Him that I wanted to learn from it all because I knew He was trying to teach me something important. My prayers would end by committing to apply what I would learn in my life so that this hard lesson would never happen again.

> ***Words of Wisdom:*** *Life's troubles are God's classroom and training ground wherein He's trying to teach you something. Therefore, don't be a reluctant student and try to take control of the classroom. Give God control. He is the ultimate instructor who genuinely loves you and cares about you. Don't ask Him*

why your troubles are happening. At that moment, you wouldn't understand His answer because you're too deeply focused on and in your trouble and pain. Instead, ask Him, "What are you trying to teach and train me to do?" Focus your mind on that question. Be a willing student. Listen attentively to His guidance and instruction. Learn, then apply it all in your life. This was the "Be Transformed and Live in Me" classroom and training ground I had entered.

~ 7 ~
LIVING A TORTURED LIFE

Over the following two months, two things occurred that, at first, I thought were great. Doug secured two jobs. But he kept most of his paychecks for himself. The little he gave barely helped to buy groceries. Another great thing was that he met and made a friend during his first job, and they would hang out together while I was working.

However, Doug was fired from both jobs after only three weeks at each job. I was thankful that he had obtained at least six paychecks and had found a friend. Nonetheless, both occurrences would prove detrimental.

What I didn't know was that he had taken each paycheck stub to various same-day fast-cash loan businesses and obtained healthy loans against them. Plus, his new friend was his drug dealer. Therefore, I would soon be faced with paying off Doug's loan debts and possibly the debt he owed his dealer friend. Repayment of the loans took many months. However, the friendship with his dealer was short-lived. Here's how that "friendship" ended.

Doug invited him over one Saturday to meet me. At that time, I had no idea that "his friend" was his dealer and was expecting payment for what he had previously provided Doug. After the introductions, our friendly conversation continued as Doug went upstairs to get something.

Moments later, the Doug who went upstairs was not the same Doug who came downstairs. He was wearing black, and his attitude had drastically changed. He was extremely agitated and angry. All heck broke loose as he started to accuse us of making out and having sex in the kitchen while he was upstairs. We were shocked by his accusations and adamantly denied them. No matter what we said, Doug refused to listen.

His friend, thinking it a bit funny, said, "Doug, you weren't even gone long enough for anything like that to happen!" Doug instantly blew up. The fight was on! The rage that filled Doug as he stormed toward his friend was much like what I'd experienced during my cigarette-smoking episode, and it scared me half to death.

A vicious fight broke out between them. As it moved from the kitchen into the living room, furniture was jarred, knocking over a lamp and the television. Vulgar, profane yells from both men filled the room as Doug pounded his friend's face and slugged his body. I stood there screaming for them to stop. I couldn't believe what was happening in my home, but what happened next scared and shocked me even more.

With brute force, Doug picked up the guy by the shirt collar, threw him against the wall, thrust his hands around his neck, and began to strangle him to death. I stood there yelling as I saw the man's face turn from a natural skin tone to pink to red, then to blue. I heard him plead for his life as he said, "Stop it. I can't breathe. You're killing me!" But Doug's rage was in control. My screams at Doug went unheeded. Without thinking, I ran over to them, forcefully wedged my body between them, dug my nails into Doug's wrists, and with a supernatural strength I didn't know I had, I pushed Doug to the floor.

Being freed from Doug's death stranglehold, the man immediately ran for the front door. Gasping for air, rubbing his neck, and yelling all kinds of vulgar words as he did, he looked back over his shoulder and yelled, "Man, I knew you were weird, but you're [fill in the blank] crazy as they get! I'm outta here!" And we never saw him again.

Doug was once again friendless. His access to drugs was gone, and his desperation to find another supplier became all he could think of. His anger at me and the world grew. And with that came the ever-mounting financial, emotional, and verbal abuse he showered upon me. His vocal threats of physical abuse increased. However, many times, instead of physically abusing me, he would physically abuse my cat. He threw or kicked her across the room many times. He was extremely cruel to her, and my concerns for my own physical well-being escalated daily.

My time in God's Word at home became extremely limited, and I only experienced it behind the closed door of the bathroom. The verbal abuse and threats of physical harm would be showered upon me if he caught me reading. Therefore, I purchased another Bible, took it to work, and dove into God's word during my lunch hour. I needed that time with God every day. It became my only private refuge with Him. During those cherished lunch hours, peace would fill me, for I knew He was with me and never abandoned me. He loved me and would always take care of me.

Yet, unspeakable fear and darkness filled me and my private life. I felt trapped within the walls of my home and the evil that surrounded me. Self-shame filled me, for I knew I was the one who had gotten myself into this predicament. Threats of harm from Doug and my self-pride kept me from sharing my circumstances with anyone except God in my prayers.

Each day, my prayers became more fervent as I asked the Lord to protect and rescue me. I could almost taste every word I prayed, saying, "Lord, forgive me. You are my God. Please hear my cry. Shield my heart and head in the battles I'm facing. You're teaching me a hard lesson, and it hurts. Oh, I'm learning the errors of my ways. Please forgive me and uphold me in your strength. Lord, hold me in your loving arms. Rescue me and get me out of the predicament I've gotten myself into."

Words of Wisdom: *Life, at times, seems to be full of pain, problems, challenges, and overwhelming darkness. However, never forget God is always near. Cry out to Him. Draw close to Him and He will draw close to you. God sees you and will hear you. He is intimately aware of every detail of your life and has promised to take care of you. There is no problem He can't resolve, no challenge too difficult for Him to handle. There's no darkness He can't drive out, and no walls He cannot tear down. He loves you and will never abandon you, no matter how badly you mess up! He is the almighty God who grants mercy and many second chances! All you must do is remain strong in your faith and, no matter what, learn to trust Him. He's a man of His word. He keeps His promises! That, once again, was a lesson He was trying to teach me.*

My private life, in every aspect, was falling apart, and my professional life didn't help at all.

Doug had no experience or understanding of anything beyond working as a regular hourly-paid employee in an eight-hour shift. My salaried position mandated nine-to-five office hours plus early morning meetings, conducting evening workshops, and attending occasional Chamber After-Hours events. Therefore, my job only fed his growing anger and inability to trust me. I was daily and quite graphically accused of having early-morning and late-night sexual affairs and encounters with men. Every attempt to rebut his accusations only aggravated the situation and produced more verbal abuse and threats of physical harm. His words were like knives plunged into my heart and bolts of fire that flamed my fears.

The only place I truly felt safe and secure was at work and within the Chamber offices. It became my safe place of refuge on Mondays through Fridays. Why? Remember that "Security Key Card" entry system the Chamber had installed in December? You know, the one I previously thought was a major pain in the ever-loving you-know-what. I was now praising God for it. The Lord had gone before me and assured me there would be no way Doug could physically get to me once I was at the office.

I kept my private life to myself, masked my despair, hid my bruises, and shared my reality with no one. Therefore, I thought my professional life continued to be strong on all levels. However, all of that didn't stop Doug's calls. By mid-February, he was calling me at least fifteen to twenty times a day on my office or cell phone. He'd always wanted to know where I was, what I was doing, and who I was with. If I didn't answer his calls, he'd leave vulgar voicemail messages accusing me of all types of things, and all heck would be waiting for me when I got home. So, although it infuriated me, I continued to answer some of his calls.

Then one day it happened. He called, and I had had enough. I slammed the receiver down and ran to the breakroom. Rose and Mark, my two "cubicle" Christian coworkers, were startled. However, that was the least of my concerns as I, in tears, angrily stormed off.

Shortly thereafter, as tears flowed down my face and my clasped fists held my bowed head, I felt Rose and Mark's comforting hands on my shoulders. They had come to the breakroom to make sure I was okay and to pray for and with me. As Rose lifted my chin so my eyes would look up at her, she said, "Nancy, you just haven't been yourself for a long time. What's going on? Please tell us."

My shame-filled response was, "I can't. I can't talk about it. I can't talk about it with anyone."

Mark compassionately stepped into the conversation and said, "Nancy, we can tell you must have an abusive man in your life. All of his ugly phone calls, the several small bruises we've seen on your arms, and your urgency to get home from work before it's too late. To us, all this stands as proof of this fact. Nancy, if you can't talk about it, it's already out of control. You've got to tell someone, talk about it, and let us help you. That is exactly what we want to do. We want to help you and pray with and for you." It was there and then that we all joined hands, and they prayed with and for me.

In that moment, I fully realized that God had put Rose and Mark in my life to be more than coworkers. They were the first earthly members of my support team who would help me get out of the destructive mess I had put myself in.

The three of us decided to gather daily by the filing cabinets in our cubicle to pray about what was happening in my life. Rose committed to researching local resources available for battered and abused women. At the time, I thought she was taking the issue a little too far, but I went along with it. They both committed to covering for me whenever I left the office early to speak with Jo and Ken or any other resource I needed for help. This assured me that my arrival home would be closer to Doug's "expected time."

My commitment was to do three important things:

- Daily continue to give my circumstances over to God, asking Him to help and protect me.
- By the end of the week, to vaguely inform my superiors of the troubles at home, that, if Doug showed up at the Chamber, he should not be allowed in, and if he called, he was only to be told I was unavailable and immediately transferred directly to the main office voicemail.
- Immediately call Jo and Ken and set up a meeting with them and tell them what was happening in my life.

Therefore, after speaking with Rose and Mark, a call was made to Jo and Ken.

I was praying they would both be available and willing to meet with me because they had recently moved. Ken had left his position as director of pastoral care at a leading area hospital in Columbus to accept the role of lead pastor at the Grove City United Methodist Church. They now lived in the parsonage next door to the church. However, Jo still operated her full-time business out of their former home, which was located close to where I lived.

There were several other reasons I hoped that they would be available. They were my shining Christian examples of living life focused on loving and serving God. I knew Jo would provide the love, input, and support my heart needed. On the other hand, I knew Ken might prove to be an answer to my prayers. He was an ordained pastor and had served several area churches. He was an active Army chaplain and counselor. Moreover, he was an experienced, well-trained EMT, and due to his most recent yet now-former position in the medical and healthcare industry, I had hoped he'd be well-connected within the medical field. I was praying that his wisdom, insights, experience, and possible resource connections would prove to be a gift from God to me. I was praising God by the end of the call, and a visit with them was confirmed for the very next day.

My resolve had started. A peace I couldn't explain filled me. Everyone's encouraging words empowered my focused strength to move forward. To this very day, I praise God that He put Rose, Mark, Jo, and Ken in my life. They and God were always there for me.

Words of Wisdom: *God is always with us, ready to lead, guide, and direct. He also created us with a desire to be connected to and with others. Therefore, no matter what is going on in your life, you need a good, strong, Christ-centered, and like-minded support system beside and behind you. It may be formed through a combination of people in your life, workplace, family, and/or involvement in a small church group. Regardless of how it is formed, you need it! Here are several reasons why:*

- *Life can be scary and cause you to feel all alone. However, if you have someone with you, you know you're not alone and feel safer because they are there to support you.*
- *The support and input they provide will serve to give you energy and encouragement to move forward in all that you do.*
- *It also makes you smarter! You learn more as you walk with others than you do walking life alone. You may never*

realize you're walking in the wrong direction or have veered off course and are headed for danger. But with other caring friends by your side, they'll help you recognize that fact, and they'll be there to help you get back on track!

Back to the reality of that day. Yes, I was ready to move forward. Yet, a degree of dread started to build because I had a workshop to conduct that evening and wouldn't get home until well after 9:00 p.m. Returning home late, especially at night, always led to what I called "The Daily Dreaded Event" because I had no idea which mood Doug would be in when I got home. Therefore, I had no certainty of what I would have to deal with and how I would be treated when I got home. Which one of Doug's two disturbing moods would be waiting for me when I walked through the door? I had to prepare myself.

In my mind, I had silently given his moods names to help me brace myself and cope with them:

The Beige Brute—He always seemed to be wearing blue jeans and beige or earth-tone clothing when he was in this mood. He could be loving and considerate. However, I had to always be on my guard because he could change from friend to foe in a split second. The foe was verbally and emotionally abusive, demanding, controlling, accusatory, indignant, and only threatened physical harm. He hardly ever followed through with his threat. Yet, he didn't trust anyone and was angry at the world all the time.

The Man in Black—He was always dressed in black. He was a brutally cruel, hateful, mean, and angrily destructive monster. Unlike the Beige Brute, this man held no loving or considerate traits. However, he did hold every other unkind and wicked trait of the Beige Brute. In addition to all of this, he would purposely create fear of physical abuse within me by throwing things at me. They would never hit me but would barely miss me. He would threaten me with physical harm and, several times, follow through with his threat. He didn't hesitate to be verbally abusive and destructive to anything, including my cat. "The Man in Black" was always ready to fight to the death over almost anything. He'd even create a cause to fight if one did not exist. There were many times I thought, "He'd rather kill me than smile at me." He, just like his other personality, didn't trust anyone and was angry at the world.

Which one would be waiting for me upon my return home?

~ 8 ~
LIVING WITH THREE IN ONE

Surprisingly, no one and nothing awaited me as I entered the house. The only light on in the entire house was the light above the kitchen range. The whole house was dark and quiet.

I called out Doug's name. He didn't respond. I checked the back patio deck and every room on the first and second floors. He was nowhere to be found. Where could he have gone? Where was he and what was he doing? My concern grew, and I started praying that he hadn't walked off and gotten himself into trouble.

Returning to the family room, I passed the door leading to the basement, and a muffled sound hit my ears. What was that sound coming from the basement? Slowly opening the door and quietly going down the steps into the dimly lit abyss of the basement, I found him. He was lying in a fetal position on the large area rug in front of the laundry room. He was mumbling and crying as he clung to a small blue blanket. Startled at the sight, I asked, "Doug, are you okay?"

Slowly straightening out and rolling over onto his back, he asked in a bewildered childlike voice, "Nancy, is that you?" I confirmed it was me. As I walked over and sat on the floor next to him, I noticed something strange. He was wearing a light blue sweatshirt and blue jogging pants. His outfit almost looked like pajamas. I had never seen him wear these clothes, act this way, or heard his voice sound the way it sounded. I was puzzled

He was still clutching the little blue blanket as he said, "Oh, Nancy, I'm so glad that you are home." With that, I thought he must have had a really bad day, was depressed, or was missing his family.

As we talked, I realized his attitude was not one of having a bad day, being depressed, or missing someone. His demeanor was that of a child—baffled, befuddled, bewildered, and confused. And my heart began to ache for him.

He told me there had been many times since he had been living with me that he'd come down into the basement. Going to the basement was something that he and his mom used to do when he lived at home. They would go to the basement to get away from his father and have private, secret talks. He then added that every time he had done this while living with me, he had hoped that either I would come home or his mom would show up. But until now, I, nor his mom, had. He was so glad I was finally home because now he could talk to me just like he and his mom used to do.

Doug began to talk and ask questions about those things he had never before wanted to ask or talk about. His desperate questions were many, and they all started with the word, "Why?" Every question he asked stemmed from what had happened to him when he was nine. Why was he the way he was? Why did his dad hate him so much? Why did his dad slam an axe into his head? Why was his dad the way he was? Why were there things that people said he did but couldn't remember doing? Why did he keep hearing voices in his head telling him to do things that he knew weren't good? Why couldn't someone help him get better? His final question was, "Isn't there anyone who can help me get better?"

My limited insight into his horrible past and not understanding the workings of an injured mind hindered my ability to answer many of his questions. Therefore, I gave him a listening ear, followed by comforting, caring, and encouraging words. However, when Doug asked his last question, I saw the Lord open the door of opportunity and jumped at the chance to tell Doug all about Ken and how he may, in some way, be able to help. I then asked him if he would be interested in and willing to talk with Ken. I also told him that if he was, I could ask Ken the very next day, as I already had a business meeting scheduled with him.

After several other questions were asked and answered, Doug agreed to talk with Ken, and we agreed on two possible dates and times for this to happen. With that, I committed to confirming Ken's willingness to talk with Doug and have him choose the day and time that would best fit his schedule.

Doug meagerly thanked me and humbly ended our conversation by saying, "Nancy, thank you for talking with me tonight. It was like I was talking to my mom. It really means a lot to me. But right now, I'm really tired and just want to go to sleep. I'm so tired. I don't even want to move. I'm going to sleep right here tonight. You go upstairs and go to bed." He curled up in a ball as he rolled onto his side. I covered him with his blanket, said good night, and quietly went upstairs. However, as I ascended the stairs out of the abyss, my mind was anything but quiet.

Loud praises to God filled my mind, for He had opened an opportunity that had accomplished many things. Doug's cry for help was heard. Information regarding Ken was shared. The offer to speak with Ken was made. Doug had agreed to it. Additionally, Doug now knew that I had a late-afternoon meeting with Ken the next day. My worries about arriving home late the next day had been washed away. My mind was rejoicing with each step I took that led me upstairs and out of the basement's abyss.

However, my thoughts changed as I settled on the couch upstairs. What kind of game was Doug playing with me? I had never seen him look like this or be in this state of mind or attitude. It was as if he were a totally different person.

That last thought jolted me. Once again, the long-ago memory of watching the movie *The Three Faces of Eve* with my dad returned to my mind. Could my dad have been wrong, and people with multiple personalities really do exist? Dad couldn't have been wrong. Yet could he have been for here I was, living a life with one person who seemed to hold not one, not two, but now three distinctively different personalities? And in that frightful moment, I decided I had to do two things before meeting with Ken.

I had to do research into this "multi-personality thing." I had to find out if it really did exist. I'd get online as soon as I got to work in the morning, connect to this relatively new search engine everyone was talking about called "Google," and see what I could find out.

Next, I needed to contact Doug's mom and find out more about his medical history and the possible past diagnosis he'd been given. If this multiple-personality phenomenon did exist, I had to ask if he'd ever been diagnosed with having it.

I'd talk to Ken about it all during our upcoming meeting. No matter if the phenomenon existed or not, my concerns and focus would be on how to get out of this horrible relationship and the mess I'd gotten myself into. This thought scared me as I desperately prayed, "Lord, help me!"

Dreadful concern built within me the next morning. My Google research confirmed that such a condition did exist, and it was known as *dissociative identity disorder* (DID).

The next thing I did was to call Doug's mom. She answered, and I identified myself. The first thing out of her mouth shocked me as she said, "Oh, dear God! Now what has he done?! Has he tried to kill someone again?" I explained that it wasn't that drastic and briefly explained all that had happened since he had arrived. She was sincerely apologetic for it all.

I told her that I needed insight into his medical history and all that they had done for him in the past. She provided a brief overview of what had happened to him at the age of nine. She then explained that his doctor had recommended several surgeries or even wanted to admit him into a long-term, possibly life-long medical facility to ensure his and others' safety. However, they could not afford the expense of doing any of these things. The only thing they could barely afford was the recommended medications. Therefore, multiple types of medications were prescribed to be taken daily for the rest of his life. They all seemed to help if Doug took them. However, he didn't like taking them, and it proved to be a daily challenge to ensure he was taking them. Therefore, it was quite easy to tell if he hadn't. One missed day and he'd start to do all kinds of strange, disturbing things.

I then asked if Doug had ever been diagnosed with DID and explained that it was often referred to as multiple personality disorder. To that, she puzzlingly chuckled and said, "No. He's just been an angry, hateful, confused, and sad person all his life." Our conversation ended as she requested to be kept informed and hung up the phone.

I hung up my receiver and immediately asked Rose and Mark to pray for me. I didn't share any details. All I said was," I'm scared half to death, and today's meeting with Jo and Ken can't come soon enough."

Hours later, I was sitting in Jo and Ken's living room, spilling out everything from the physical, emotional, and financial abuse I was experiencing to the ongoing fears and threats of more physical abuse brought upon me by the two strong moods Doug displayed.

I shared all the information I had received from Doug's mom. However, I did not share anything about the conversation Doug and I had in the basement the night before. I was still confused by that experience and thought he might be playing another cruel game with my emotions.

Sharing all of this was both humiliating and yet cleansing at the same time. Jo lovingly stated that they both suspected something was drastically wrong and thanked me for finally sharing it all with them. When asked, Ken confirmed that people with multiple personalities did exist and confirmed his knowledge of the disorder. He then added that it was a confusing and potentially dangerous disorder for not only the individual but also for those within the person's life. To that, only my mind responded, "You're not kidding, it does!"

Ken confirmed his willingness to talk with Doug. A call was immediately made to Doug, and all was confirmed by the end of the call. Their meeting would be held at 6:00 p.m. the following night at my house. They both agreed that I should not be home during their talk and that Ken would call me when they were done. Ken and I had hoped that a more open conversation would occur in my absence.

Jo and Ken continued to share their deep, heartfelt concerns, loving care, and support as I prepared to leave. It humbled me greatly as I wondered why I had waited so long to share it all with them. Hand in hand, Jo walked me to my car. Long, loving hugs were shared as she said a prayer of protection over me before I headed home.

Wiping tears from my face as I turned into the driveway, I prayed that all would be fine when I entered the house. And it was. The house was quiet. Once again, the kitchen light was the only light on in the house. I called out his name, and he replied, "I'm upstairs in bed watching TV." I told him I had some office work to do before coming to bed. He was fine with that as he was tired and would probably fall asleep soon. I was fine with that, too, and slept on the couch that night.

The next morning, during our office prayer time together, Rose and Mark were updated on the outcomes of my meeting with Jo and Ken. They each said a prayer for me and vowed to cover for me if I had or wanted to leave the office a little early. Later that afternoon, I accepted their offer. They both, once again, said a prayer for me as I left.

"The Beige Brute" was waiting for me when I got home. He greeted me by accusingly asking, "What are you doing at home? It's a little early, isn't it? Don't you have one of your 'hot meetings' to go to with whatever his name is?" And with that, his ongoing argumentative attempts began. Trying to make him understand there were no other "men" in my life other than him was impossible.

Finally giving up the fight, I said, "Doug, I'm home because you have a meeting with Ken, my brother-in-law, tonight. Last night on the phone, you agreed to talk with him, and he'll be over to talk to you in about an hour. Don't you remember? I'm home now to make sure you're ready for your meeting with him because I'll be leaving before he gets here. We all agreed to that last night. Don't you remember?"

Doug looked at me as though he didn't know what I was talking about, but said, "Well, if that's the case, do you know what he wants to talk to me about?

My reply was, "You said you needed help, and he agreed to talk to you."

His reply was, "Well then, if that's the case, I guess I'd better go upstairs and get ready for him." Grumbling and muttering to himself, he turned and stormed upstairs to take a shower and get ready.

Over thirty minutes later, Doug was still upstairs, hopefully getting ready. I yelled up to him that I was leaving and said, "Goodbye." There was no response, so I yelled my goodbyes one more time and left, pleadingly praying to God that their 6:00 p.m. meeting would go well and that Ken would have some insights to share when I returned.

I went to a local restaurant, ate my dinner, and read a book until I received Ken's call. Their meeting had lasted over an hour and a half. Surely Ken would have something to share with me.

Ken was the only one in the living room when I returned. Out of concern, I asked where Doug was. Ken advised that he had gone upstairs because he was tired and wanted to be alone. I then asked what he thought of my concerns. Ken's reply was, "Nancy, he certainly has some problems, and he's afraid and worried about what it all means. I agree with you. Doug does need psychological help. I'll see who I can connect him up with."

I heard every word Ken said. However, the two words that stuck in my mind were "afraid" and "worried." Those two words didn't fit the controlling, accusatory, angry, mean, and abusive Doug who had been living with me since the beginning of the year. Therefore, I took a chance, and my next questions were, "Who do you think you were talking to? What was his demeanor?"

His replied, "Nancy, I felt as though I was talking to a scared little boy, probably no older than nine years old."

His answer left me dumbfounded, speechless, and angry. Although speechless, my brain was screaming, "Doug, what kind of game are you playing with me? What are you trying to pull off, and who are you trying to fool? Come on, a scared nine-year-old boy?" However, my brain froze with that last thought. A nine-year-old boy? That's how old Doug was when his dad slammed an axe into his head and severely damaged his brain.

I looked at Ken and asked, "What was Doug wearing tonight, and where is he now? Ken replied, "A light blue jogging outfit, and he went upstairs because he said he was tired and needed to lie down."

My brain, once again, silently pleaded, *Oh Lord, help me!*

Ken told me to give him a call if "anything came up" or if I needed anything. He also promised to follow through on his commitment to touch base with one of the hospital's qualified psychologists. As he left and shut the door behind him, I thanked him for his willingness to assist me and help Doug.

The house was totally quiet. I stood there in the silence that surrounded me and talked to the Lord, saying, "Lord, I'm scared. What am I going to do? Please, hear my prayers and help me. The thought of living with a person who may have multiple personalities scares me half to death. I thought there might be two. However, now there might be three. Dear Lord, be with me. I beg You, keep me safe. Be with me and help me get through this." The quietness of my environment fell on me, and I asked, "Lord, what should I do?" And with that question, I heard His answer, *Go upstairs and see if he's okay.* So that's what I did.

The bedroom door was only half closed. The dim light from the bedroom lit my path up the stairway. I was somewhat mystified as I entered the room. Doug was curled up in bed, clutching his pillow. He turned toward me and quietly said, "Nancy, I'm so glad you're home." I saw that he was wearing the same blue sweatshirt and pants he had on the night before. His demeanor, speech pattern, and even his facial features reminded me of the person I had met in the basement. As we talked, I realized that the man I was looking at and talking to was not, in any sense of the word, "The Beige Brute" nor "The Man in Black." He was a defenseless, bewildered, and confused little boy who desperately sought answers and craved a resolution to his problems.

Our conversation was brief. Doug said he was tired of talking, and his brain hurt. He just wanted to go back to sleep. I obliged him, granted his wish, and told him I'd sleep downstairs on the couch to ensure he'd get a good night's sleep. As I turned off the light, I told him I'd see him in the morning. My heart ached for him as I descended the stairs and said a silent prayer for him.

Turbulent thoughts of everything that had happened since January spun through my mind. They were all focused on one thing. The man who lived with me and had become a part of my life.

"The Beige Brute," "The Man in Black," and now, "Little Boy Blue." He was a bewildered, baffled, and confused little boy. All three were within one body. They were the "Three in One Doug."

None of them fully trusted anyone, knew how to love someone, or knew what true love was.

As I prayed for the Lord's protection and fell asleep on the couch, little did I know that in the following days, "The Beige Brute" would become more controlling and emotionally brutal. "The Man in Black" would become even more prevalent and physically dangerous. And I'd never see "Little Boy Blue" again, even though I knew he existed.

"The Beige Brute" awaited me the next night as I returned home from work. He was not in a good mood. The first words out of his mouth were accusatory questions. "Why are you late? Where have you been? Who were you with this time?"

A verbally abusive argument broke out as I, in tears, tried to explain I wasn't late, I'd been at the office all day, and that I hadn't "been" with anyone. I was on my knees begging him to believe me when he finally gave up. He took me in his arms, hugged me, and said he was sorry. He blamed it all on having a headache and that "something" inside of him was going wrong. He didn't like how he was feeling and didn't know what was causing him to feel that way. All he knew was he needed his medications to make it all stop, and his medications were long gone. He then looked at me and said, "Nancy, I need help."

Thinking this was the breakthrough I'd been praying for, I mentioned the conversations he and Ken had the night before. However, Doug had no recollection of any of it. I shared how Ken had told him that he could hook him up with helpful resources, such as psychologists and mental health facilities in the area, to get the help he needed. With that, Doug angrily blew up and said, "What! Do you all think I'm crazy? I ain't going to no looney bin!" As he ranted on, I tried to explain Ken's offer to help, but it only made things worse. Doug's rage exploded.

Out of fear, I ran upstairs to the bathroom and locked the door behind me. He came up later to apologize, but I didn't say a word or open the door. As he walked away, I swore to myself to never again mention Ken's offer to help him. And, as I fell asleep on the bathroom floor, I fervently prayed and pleaded with the Lord to keep me safe and to get him out of my life. That bathroom prayer would become my constant plea to the Lord throughout the days to come.

"The Beige Brute" or "The Man in Black" were the only ones to show their faces during the next two days. Once again, I felt as though I was walking on broken glass. My home environment was emotionally abusive, unstable, and turbulent.

The only safe place I had was at the office. The only people I vaguely kept informed were Jo, Ken, Rose, and Mark, and I thanked God they all continued to cover me with their prayers. However, I never told my parents nor my daughter, Elizabeth, about what was happening in my life. Elizabeth still lived in Arkansas, and I didn't want to worry her nor my parents about what was going on in my terrified home life. And everyone who I had confided in knew I wanted to keep it that way.

However, what happened the next night made me start wondering if God was hearing my prayers or those who were praying for me.

"The Man in Black" was waiting for me that night as I returned home from conducting an evening workshop. He was angry and complaining about everything under the sun. There was no appeasing him. He simply wanted to be mad at me and the world. All kinds of angry words and degrading accusations were flying out of his mouth. He would not listen to any reasoning of why or where I had been. He began taking his anger out on my cat. He picked her up and kicked her, like a football, across the family room toward the fireplace. I pleaded with him to stop and calm down as I ran to rescue and console her. That made him even angrier, and he accused me of caring for "the stupid [blankety-blank] cat" more than I cared about him.

With cat in arms, I turned to rebut his accusation, but not a word came out of my mouth. Instead, I dropped the cat and fearfully froze. "The Man in Black" was angrily charging toward me like a football player ready to make a shoulder tackle. And that he did! His tackle knocked the wind out of me as I went flying backward through the air like the Wile E. Coyote in a Looney Tunes and Merrie Melodies cartoon. My head slammed into the edge of the brick fireplace hearth as I landed. I could hardly breathe or move.

The pain was excruciating. My head was spinning, and blood was seeping out from the gash on my right temple.

Doug came running over, looked down at me, and asked if I was okay. I only moaned, but my brain was shouting, *What?! Am I okay? You just tackled me and flew me through the room! I'm hurt, can't breathe, and bleeding. Am I okay? What do you think?*

However, as I looked up at him, I realized that although he was dressed in black, it wasn't "The Man in Black" standing over me. His physical demeanor and his verbal mannerisms had changed. The man looking down on me and speaking to me was Doug "The Beige Brute." His personality had switched from "The Man in Black" back into "The Beige Brute" in seconds! The Brute pulled me up and held me in his arms as he checked out my head. I lost count of the tons of times he said, "I'm sorry" and "I promise, it'll never happen again." I didn't reply because I didn't believe it for a minute.

My mind was whirling as I broke loose from his hold and staggered over to sit in a chair. He got a bag of frozen peas from the freezer, wrapped it in a damp rag, came back to me, and applied it to my head.

I'll never forget what I heard and saw not even a minute later. Looking directly at me, Doug aggravatingly said, "Well, at least I didn't beat you. I didn't even lay a hand on you. You stupid fool. You just fell and hit your head." Doug then turned and "The Man in Black, dressed like The Beige Brute, went upstairs for the night.

The house fell silent, but my brain was screaming, *Lord, please hear my prayers! I know You're there and listening to me. I'm begging and will keep on begging You, keep me safe and get him out of my life!* Those thoughts and my pleas drifted through my mind as the couch, once again, became my safe sleeping place.

Words of Wisdom: *No matter what you're going through, never stop praying. The Bible says He hears our prayers and He keeps His promises. God promises in Matthew 7:7–8, "Ask and it shall be given you; seek, and you will find, knock and the door will be opened unto you." Keep knocking on His door! He will answer and open the doors. However, when you ask, you must believe because James 1:6-7 says, "But when you ask, you must believe and not doubt, because the one who doubts is like a wave of the sea, blown and tossed by the wind. That person should not expect to receive anything from the Lord."*

There is then one last thing you need to do. Don't worry about it! Philippians 4:6–7(NLT) says, "Don't worry about anything; instead, pray about everything. Tell God what you need and thank him for all he has done. Then you will experience God's peace, which exceeds anything we can understand. His peace will guard your hearts and minds as you live in Christ Jesus." This process of asking in prayer, believing He'll do it, and not worrying about it works! How do I know? Read on and you'll find out!

Getting ready for work the next morning was a cosmetic chore and a disaster. My temple was swollen, and my right eye was black and blue. I did my best to camouflage it all. However, it was to no avail. Mark and Rose's first statements to me were, "What in the world happened to your eye?!"

A sketchy overview of what had happened was given as we gathered for our morning prayer time. After the "amens" were said, they encouraged me to immediately call Ken to see if he was available to talk. I called Ken and told him I needed help and needed to talk to one of his qualified psychologist buddies. He was available to meet with me that very afternoon. Without even asking him, Mark committed to covering my client cases for me, and I took the day off. As I left, Rose interjected that she was going to start gathering information regarding safe housing for battered and abused women in the area. I thanked her and said, "All I know right now is that I'm moving forward, and the strength that God will give me is going to help me get through it all."

Words of Wisdom: *When troubles and challenges come, you have a choice. Choosing to view your life through the lens of your circumstances will make it appear hopeless. However, if you look through the lens of God's power and His overwhelming love for you, trust will flood your soul and displace the lies of fear mounting within you. Move forward and fear not!*

~ 9 ~
FRIGHTFUL INSIGHTS AND DIRECTIVES

My meeting with Ken was most beneficial. Within two days, I was sitting in the office of one of the hospital's leading psychologists for a free session with him, which lasted well over an hour.

He confirmed that Ken had previously filled him in on my situation, concerns, and fears. However, before proceeding, he had some questions, which might provide him with additional insights into what Ken had already shared with him and what I was facing.

Here are the "Has Doug ever or consistently" questions he asked. An emphatic "Yes!" was my reply to all of them except for his last question.

- Limited where you could go and whom you were allowed to see?
- Demand you make major life changes?
- Tell you not to talk to anyone about what happens at home, to keep a bad secret, or to lie for him?
- Stop you from talking about a certain topic?
- Disrespect you in your relationship with him?
- Been verbally or physically abusive toward you?
- Been dishonest or shown any traits of being dishonest?

- Totally shut himself down and refused to communicate with you?
- Make you doubt how others feel or care about you?
- Belittle you, your opinion, or made you feel unimportant?
- Been unfaithful to you?

I slightly chuckled as I answered "No" to his last question and added, "Are you kidding? It seems as though I have been his whole life. He has no other."

He looked at me and said, "Okay, now it's your turn. Fill me in on what's been happening, things you've seen and experienced in your relationship with Doug since he arrived in December."

During that time, I shared what I knew of Doug's terrible life history and shared what his mother had told me during my phone conversation with her. I described the three different personalities by the mood names I'd given them. I shared what I'd faced and the horrific, frightening experiences I'd had with them all. I also shared the fact that Doug had run out of all medications by the end of January and added that his adamant refusal to get any medical help hadn't helped his or my situation. I was an emotional wreck by the time I finished and asked, "So, Doctor, what do you think based on all I've shared?

The doctor gave me a serious look and said, "Nancy, we're not only meeting today so you gain some insight into Doug's possible condition, but more importantly, to help you. So, before I answer your question, let me ask you some questions."

His first question was, "With whom have you shared any of this?" I named four people. His second was, "When did you share it?" I informed him that it had only been within the last several weeks. His last question was twofold: "Why did you wait so long to talk to anyone about it, and why haven't you left the situation you're living in?"

I answered the second part of his question first, and it was quite direct. I hadn't left because I was the one who belonged in my home. He didn't. If I did leave, I would be leaving behind and possibly lose everything I had. Plus, landlord troubles could have arisen if I had left, since Doug had nowhere else he could afford to go.

However, answering the first part of his question was emotionally tough for me. I knew I had to be transparent. Tears immediately began to well up in my eyes and trickled down my face as I answered.

My deep shame and guilt were shared. I felt I had brought it upon myself because of the choices I'd made during my Thanksgiving in Arkansas. It was all my fault. My many fears were also shared. They included: being physically abused or causing a frightful argument if I didn't do what he wanted, the opinion of others if they found out what was happening to me, and people not believing me if I did tell them. I told the doctor I just didn't want to talk to anybody about it because I thought that eventually I could handle it or get it all under control on my own.

His response was like an echo in my head, as I had recently heard something similar spoken to me. "Nancy, none of this is your fault. Your fears, although justifiable in your own mind, have prevented you from moving forward and talking to someone about it. Therefore, when it comes to emotional and physical abuse, I want you to remember this. Not wanting to talk about it is a sign that it's already out of control. However, telling someone about it is the first major step in taking control of it."

> ***Words of Wisdom:*** *If you are reading this and are presently in an emotionally and/or physically abusive relationship, tell someone you trust about it. God has put that trusted friend in your life for such a time as this. Not wanting to talk about it is definitely a sign that your situation is out of control. Take control and tell that caring and trusted friend about it. It is the first major step you can take in doing so.*

The doctor then proceeded with the session, focusing on Doug. He was very professional and stated that a true diagnosis could not be given because he had not met with Doug. But, given all the research studies done by the Mao Clinic, the Cleveland Clinic, and McLean Hospital, it did sound as though I was living with a man who had a serious mental health condition. He confirmed what I'd already suspected: Doug had DID and could very well have three separate personalities. These three personalities were designated as alter identities.

He continued to explain the reasoning behind his conclusion based on the published research done by the resources he had noted:

- Most mental health professionals believe that the underlying cause of dissociative disorders is chronic trauma in childhood and throughout their lives. Some of these traumas include repeated physical, sexual, and emotional abuse or neglect. Personality traits are created to keep individuals safe and help them cope with life. This would explain Doug's three different personalities:
- The Beige Brute—His troubled teen years and early adult life.
- The Man in Black—Doug's years spent fighting to survive life in prison.
- Little Boy Blue—The devastatingly abused nine-year-old boy who is now puzzled, searching for answers, and hearing voices

in his head. (Which are most likely his other two personalities conversing with each other or with him directly.)

- "Alter" identities tend to have their own postures, gestures, distinctive ways of talking, and preferences in the clothes they wear.
- Each personality reveals itself and controls its own behavior and thoughts. When the different personalities change, it is called *switching*. This transition can be sudden and startling. However, family members can usually tell when a person switches.
- Triggers that cause these switches can range from stress, strong emotions, senses, special events, substance abuse, and specific troubling situations.
- Other symptoms of DID that can be revealed within the various personalities include anxiety, depression, self-destructive behavior, substance misuse or abuse, and memory gaps. Yet, the most drastic symptom is known as "dissociative rage," which is medically defined as a state of pathologically angry behavior that can occur when someone is chronically dissociated or repressing anger. He explained that this dissociation is a defense mechanism that involves disconnecting from reality, thoughts, feelings, memories, or surroundings. It leads to frequent uncontrolled outbursts of extreme emotions, including anger and rage. Simply put, they have an extremely low anger threshold. The alter personality often uses rage to protect itself from stressful

situations or traumatic experiences.

The doctor then shared one more analysis. He based this analysis on the totality of what Ken and I had shared. He looked at me and said, "It also sounds as though the two stronger personalities Doug holds are showing extreme signs of being psychopathic." The doctor's reasoning behind this included the following:

- Psychopaths show less empathy and remorse than other people. They may lie, cheat, steal, and get outrageously angry at you. However, at times they may also seem friendly and unremarkable, normal.
- They do not experience fear as others do. When confronted with a dreadful situation, they tend to react with a strategy to simply get out of it.
- A psychopathic person doesn't feel anything because they are unable to process emotion and empathy. Without these basic human emotions, they tend not to care about their family members and often live with them only to achieve a good life. They'll lie to ensure their good life continues and say, "What? Of course, I love you!"

I sat there quietly for several moments, my mind running through all the things the doctor had shared. I'd been through and seen them all. Taking a deep breath, I asked the doctor, "So, doctor, what do you see and what should I do?"

The doctor leaned back in his plush office chair, put his elbows on the arms of the chair, clasped his hands together, and pensively tapped his index fingers to his lips. After several moments, he responded to my question.

"Nancy, let me answer the first part of your question. What do I see? I see the 'Ides of March' coming upon you." I knew many people referred to it but didn't know what it meant. So, I asked and he proceeded to explain. "The Ides of March refers to ancient Roman times and the reign of Julius Caesar. Caesar thought he had loyal friends, but they plotted against him and killed him on March 15, which is now known as 'The Ides of March.'

"So, Nancy, in your case, what do I see? I see myself sitting at home within the next several weeks listening to the evening news. The breaking news of the day is that there had been multiple murders and a suicide in your area. A man killed the woman he was living with. However, before he killed her, he went over to her relatives' home and killed them first. After that, he came back, killed her, and then committed suicide. The woman was you. The relatives were Jo and Ken. And Doug was the man who killed all of you and then committed suicide. That's what I see."

Shock, fear, and panic mounted within me. I instantly felt nauseous and sick to my stomach as my heart dropped to the floor. Past thoughts of hearing news reports like this flew through my head. I never could understand the reasoning behind the killing of the family members. I looked at the doctor as I began to cry and said, "I can understand why he would want to kill me. However, I can't fathom why he would want to kill Jo and Ken."

His reply was straightforward: "It's because he sees them as the reason and major culprits behind making you not want him in your life."

My tearful retort was, "But doctor, they've had nothing to do with it. It's all him. He himself is the reason."

The doctor's gentle response was, "And that is what makes cases, as I've just shared with you, so sad and drastically devastating.

The doctor patiently and quietly gave me several moments to calm myself. Taking a deep breath, I somberly looked up at him, and he took that as his cue to continue.

His facial expression showed great concern as he said, "Now, to answer your last question of what you should do. Nancy, get out of there as soon as possible! You are in grave danger of what I just shared happening to you. Get out! Go somewhere where you'll be safe. That place cannot be Jo and Ken's. Even though you've said Doug has only been over to their home once and paid no attention to how you took him there, you can't run the risk of him somehow remembering. Let's pray he never does. So let me repeat, for your sake and theirs, that safe place cannot be Jo and Ken's home. You need to go somewhere where absolutely no one will know the location of your safe place. I truly believe lives are at stake."

The terror of it all settled deep within me as I left his office. The thought that Jo & Ken might be murdered because of the stupid Thanksgiving choices I'd made in Arkansas fueled my fear and heartache. Jo and Ken had nothing to do with it. They had only tried to comfort and help me.

I felt the overwhelming burden of my bad choices crashing down upon me. I had gotten into this mess all by myself. However, I knew I couldn't get myself or anyone else out of it all by myself. I needed help to prevent the doctor's scenario from becoming reality.

My desperate prayers to the Lord began as I left the doctor's office. They all centered around the following things: (a) asking God to forgive me, (b) helping me find that safe place where no one would know where I was, (c) strengthening me to expeditiously move forward to escape a deadly tragedy from occurring, (d) keeping all those involved safe from harm throughout the pending escape process, and (e) claiming and declaring, in the Name of Jesus Christ, that no one was going to harm or kill Jo, Ken, or me on the Ides of March, which was only a week away. Time was of the essence.

Words of Wisdom: *We were not created to carry the burdens and messes of life all on our own. The Lord wants to and will meet us in our messes and carry our burdens for us. All we have to do is stand firm in Him as we call out and submit everything to Him. Psalm 55:22 (NLT) says, "Give your burdens to the LORD, and he will take care of you. He will not permit the godly to slip and fall." God proved it to Moses and the Israelites when He parted the Red Sea, to Daniel in the lions' den, to Shadrach, Meshach, and Abednego in the fiery furnace, and to King David when King Saul and others were trying to kill him. Our God is the same God that King David praised, saying, "Praise be to the Lord, to God our Savior, who daily bears our burdens" Psalm 68:19.*

God has been, is, and will always be consistently true to who He is. He always keeps His promises. He is our provider and a constant source of comfort and strength. He is the One who continually takes care of us and stoops down to meet us in our messes. He's the One who carries us out of the darkness of our troubled lives. He is our burden bearer and our ever-present help in times of need.

My dear friend, if you are currently carrying a heavy burden that weighs you down, or if you're attempting to change a life circumstance that seems almost humanly impossible to accomplish alone, I implore you to stop! Our God specializes in carrying heavy burdens, solving problems, and turning the impossible into glorious possibilities! He is there for you. He is simply waiting for you to stop trying to do it all on your own and submit it all to Him. Ask Him to lead, guide, and direct you, and then get out of His way and give Him control. You'll be amazed at what He can and will do for you. I know and speak the truth about that fact because He was about to reveal His magnificent, mighty hands at work for me.

~ 10 ~
THE IDES OF MARCH ESCAPE

The memories of the following week are, at best, blurred together. All I know now is that God was guiding, directing, loving, and protecting me throughout it all. Here's what I recall.

I went to work the next day. Thanks to the information Rose had gathered, I made my first lunch-hour phone call to the Lutheran Social Services of Central Ohio's LSS CHOICES. It was the county's only program that provided temporary shelter for victims of domestic violence. The shelter's location was unpublished. Therefore, if I didn't tell anybody where I was, no one in the outside world would know where I was! Plus, their services also included a 24-hour crisis and information hotline, counseling, support groups, and legal community advocates for those impacted by domestic violence.

I was excited and hopeful as I made my first call and shared all the details of my situation and circumstances with them. However, my first contact with them yielded no immediate results. All rooms were occupied, and they advised me to call back daily in case something became available later in the week. Their directives were followed to the "T." I went to work every day, diligently completed my job responsibilities, and called them every day.

Daily calls were also made to my twin sister and my youngest sister, Jodie, to keep them both updated on everything. Jodie and her family lived in a community approximately twenty-five miles from Columbus, and she had also offered to help in any way possible when the time came.

Nightly, I coped with living in an increasingly dangerous and tumultuously terrifying home environment. Given any chance I could get, I secretly gathered clothes and packed them in a bag and suitcase hidden in the hall coat closet. I believed my escape would happen and claimed my safe place would soon become available. No matter what, I would be ready.

The opportunity to ask Jodie for help came one night toward the end of the week. "The Man in Black" was waiting for me when I arrived home from work. For some unknown reason, he was in an uproariously angry and ugly state of mind. Every attempt to reason with him or calm him was fruitless. He was ranting about everything under the sun and started breaking and throwing anything he could get his hands on at me. As his anger grew, he turned his rage not only on me but on my cat as well. All types of vulgar words spewed out of his mouth as he bent over, picked her up by the tail, flung her around his head, forcefully threw her against the wall, and yelled, "And get rid of this dang cat!"

In that shocking moment, I realized one important thing I had overlooked. LSS CHOICES didn't allow pets to be housed within the shelter. I had to find a safe place for my cat, too. Tears were running down my face as I ran over to pick up and console my dazed cat. I begged Doug to stop, but my begging only fueled his anger. And that's when I thought of Jodie. She was a pet owner and loved cats and dogs.

Acting like I was surrendering to Doug's demands, I told him I'd get rid of the cat and call Jodie, my sister he had never met, to see if she would take her. Doug immediately handed me the phone and told me to call her. The call was made, and thanks to her knowledge of what was going on in my life, she readily agreed. By the end of the call, plans had been made to deliver my cat to her the next night, which was Friday.

As I drove to work Friday morning, prayers of praise were lifted to God for providing a safe and loving home for my cat. Fervent prayer requests were also made that He would soon open doors and provide a safe place for me as well. It was Friday morning, and the coming Wednesday was "The Ides of March," which was only six days away.

Rose, Mark, and a cup of coffee awaited me as I walked into our office cubicle. After an update on last night's events, we gathered back by the filing cabinets for our daily prayer time. Their daily prayers and caring concern for me never ceased.

My lunch break finally arrived, and I made the daily call to LSS CHOICES. However, this time I was not disappointed. I hung up, rejoicing and praising God! A room and bed would be waiting for me on Wednesday, March 15th! I immediately claimed it as mine. They then provided detailed instructions for Wednesday. I agreed to follow them all without hesitation. My Ides of March escape would be activated in six days!

My spirit was also rejoicing in the Lord that Friday night as I prepared to take my cat to Jodie's. I not only packed up all my cat's belongings but some of mine as well. God had opened the opportunity for me to, unbeknownst to Doug, load my belongings into the car as well as my cat's. Preparation for my own escape to a safe place was underway. As I loaded the car, Psalm 138:8 (NLT) came to mind. It states that "The Lord will work out his plans for my life—for your faithful love, O Lord, endures forever." He hadn't abandoned me!! Matter of fact, He had made my escape plan even better than what I'd planned!

A call was made to Jo while at Jodie's. They were both updated on the day's glorious events, and a plan of action for Wednesday night was discussed and agreed upon. A huge hug and tearful kisses were given to Jodie as I left. We both knew I wouldn't be seeing or talking to her until Doug was out of my life, and who knew how long that might take.

Memories of the next five days are mixed and far between. There are only two things I truly remember. The first is seizing every God-given opportunity to secretly gather all I would need in the future, pack it, and hide my suitcase and bag in the hall coat closet. The other memory occurred the night before my escape. It is still quite vivid in my mind.

"The Beige Brute was waiting for me Tuesday night when I got home from work. He was angry at the world and ready to pick a fight with it or anyone who got in his way. Everything got on his nerves. His emotions were running rampant. All my attempts to calm him were only minimally successful.

By the end of the night, all I wanted to do was fall asleep on the couch. I needed to be ready to put Wednesday's plan into action. However, Doug had other plans in mind. He sat down beside me and said, "Okay, I'm going upstairs to wash up and then I'm coming down and taking you to bed with me. And whether you want to or not, we're going to make love tonight."

I sat there frozen in place. As he went upstairs, I began to pray. "Lord, the last thing I want to do is go to bed with him, let alone make love with him. It wouldn't be love. It would be rape. Lord, I don't even want him to touch me. I'm scared, Lord. I don't want anything bad to happen to me tonight. Please help me. If he forces me to go to bed with him, I'll feel as though I'm being raped by and sleeping with the devil. Lord, help me, please! It's in Your name I pray. Amen."

The phone rang the very second after I'd said "Amen." It was Jo. She wanted to know how I was doing. I told her what had just happened and my fear of what might happen if I refused. She abruptly interrupted me and said, "Nancy, whatever you do, don't go to bed with him tonight! You'll be sleeping with the devil if you do."

I was shocked by her words because I hadn't made any mention of the prayer I had just prayed. However, I immediately did so. We both agreed that it was a sign from God telling me to fear not, remain in peace, know that He is in control, and not go to bed with Doug. God was in control. Our conversation ended with a united prayer for a safe and successful escape tomorrow.

Moments later, Doug was coming downstairs but abruptly stopped halfway down, and said, "Honey, for some reason I'm not feeling good all of a sudden. I think I'm going to get sick. I'm just going to go to bed. You can sleep down here if you want."

I quietly and meagerly said, "Okay." However, I wish you could have heard my joyful praises and thanks to God screaming in my head! As Doug turned to go back upstairs, I told him it was probably for the best, as I would be leaving early for a morning meeting and wouldn't want to wake him. I heard the bedroom door shut and immediately jumped up and did a little happy dance to God.

That night, as I fell asleep, my prayer was much like King David's as he prayed, saying, "But my eyes are fixed on you, Sovereign Lord; in you, I take refuge, do not give me over to death. Keep me safe from the traps set by evildoers, from the snares they have laid for me. Let the wicked fall into their own nets, while I pass by in safety," (Psalm 141:8–10, NLT). I felt God's loving arms around me and knew He was in control.

Before leaving the house on Wednesday morning, I double-checked my suitcase and bag hidden in the closet. They were found undisturbed and waiting for my return later that night. I was off and running! Much had to be accomplished both professionally and personally before I left work that day.

During my break, I called my local police department, told them about my situation, requested a police escort to my home, and advised them of the approximate time I would be arriving at the police station later that day. Without hesitation, they agreed and assured me my escort would be waiting for me.

During my lunch hour, I called my contact at LSS CHOICES and confirmed the plan of action they had detailed for me to follow. An update call to Jo was also made to confirm the approximate time I'd be over to say goodbye before heading to the police station for my escort home. It was a go, and the countdown for my Wednesday," Ides of March" escape was on!

Unlike Julius Caesar, I wasn't going to lose my life on this day. Instead, I was taking steps to save it, and I knew God was with me every step of the way.

The time finally came to leave the office and head for Jo's. Rose, Mark, and I gathered back by the filing cabinets to pray. Each of them said a prayer asking the Lord to strengthen me, be with me, and keep me safe in all things that were to come. I hugged them both as I left, thanking them for their prayers and all they had helped me accomplish.

Much love and many tearful hugs were shared during my short visit with Jo. I told her I would call her later that night to let her know I was safe. Both of our hearts ached, knowing we would not see each other for an indefinite time, and that she would have no idea where I was. However, I did tell her she could call me at the office anytime if need be. Before I left, she, too, said a prayer for me, which was followed by many tearful goodbyes.

Two police officers were waiting for me when I arrived at the police station. They advised me of what to expect, saying, "Let us do all the talking for you. He'll be surprised. He'll not understand what's going on, but we will tell him. As you gather your stuff, he will beg you to stay and promise it will never happen again. Don't listen to his begging. We all know it will happen again if you stay. The only thing you should say is 'I'm leaving.' Keep gathering your stuff. The only other thing you should say is, "Officers, I'm ready to leave." We'll then safely escort you back to your car, follow you as you leave, and stay in the area to ensure he doesn't attempt to follow you after you leave."

The officers followed me home, and that's exactly how it all went down. I was a nervous wreck throughout the entire process. The officers escorted me back to my car, and I drove away, leaving behind everything I hadn't packed. I was heading for my next destination. It would connect me with those who would take me to my final yet unknown destination, where I knew my safe haven awaited me.

The sun was setting when I arrived at the connection destination. Following the instructions they had given, I walked to the front of a building where I waited for them to arrive. A short time later, a car slowly approached, and the driver asked if I was Nancy. I replied, "Yes." With that, they introduced themselves and told me they would take me back to my car. Once there, we transferred my things into their car, and as we did, they explained their last two directives.

Long-term parking anywhere near the shelter was strictly prohibited. Therefore, I was to follow them to a safe place where, at no expense to me, I had to park my car for what may become the long term. Once my car was safely parked, they would take me to my final destination.

Their directives were followed, and later that night, I entered the unpublished location of my safe haven and refuge, CHOICES.

> **Words of Wisdom:** *In times of trouble or despair, stand firm in your faith. Trust God and pray! Your prayers are powerful because of "Who" is listening to them! God hears and listens to your prayers. He will answer. Therefore, trust God, despite any seemingly impossible situation or trouble you may face. He is powerful and the master of turning the impossible into possible! You are not alone nor powerless in your problems when you pray, believe, and realize that God's power is bigger and greater than any problem you're facing.*

~ 11 ~
A PLACE CALLED CHOICES

Have you ever experienced something that at first scared you half to death, but, in the end, drastically changed your life forever? That's what happened to me as I was escorted into the dimly lit entrance of my safe place. It was a life and living environment that I'd never experienced before. Many women of all races and lifestyles were milling or sitting in the commons area, where several children were also playing. As my escort led me to the office, I remember thinking, *Wow, Lord! All these women and children are here for the same reason I am. We're all victims of abuse.*

Introductions to my case worker were made. She signed me in and assigned me to the room I would be sharing with one other woman. She then covered all the "dos and don'ts," and I agreed to abide by them as well as all the duties expected of becoming a CHOICES resident. She then escorted me to my room. As we entered my assigned room, she advised that all the clothes I couldn't get into the small chest of drawers or hang, including all my valuables, should be kept in my locked suitcase and stored under my bed for safekeeping. While unpacking, I thanked God for my safe place and requested that He also help keep my stuff safe.

As the caseworker left the room, she told me that once all was unpacked and safely stored, I could either remain in my room for some quiet time or return to the commons area to meet some of the other women. At first, I chose to sit quietly on my bed. However, the anxious energy of the day soon took over. I needed to be around people, so I headed for the commons area.

My heart ached as I entered the room. The environment was a mix of the joyful noise of innocent children playing and the troubled, downcast, broken spirits of women who had been victimized by their abusers. Several women had vivid signs of their injuries. Rough and tough attitudes mingled among those who were meek and mild. However, none of them were dressed in business attire as I was. Therefore, even though I was a victim just like them, the feeling of being "out of place" overwhelmed me. What was I going to say if someone said something about it?

It was at that very moment that a lady stopped me by sticking out her leg, looked up at me, snarled at me, and asked, "What the heck are you doing here?"

I was shocked and unprepared to respond, so I asked, "What do you mean?"

She sat there with a look of disgust building on her face and sneered, "Well, look at ya, all suited up and professional-looking. What the hell are you doing here?"

I quickly asked the Lord to give me the words, took a deep breath, and gently replied matter-of-factly, "Well, I guess I'm here as living proof that any woman can be a victim of abuse. And right now, I'm praising God and thankful that such a place as CHOICES exists. I bet you are too." With that, the lady immediately became quiet, bent her head, and mumbled that she was sorry. Her apology was accepted with a slight nod of my head and a tender smile. Having done so, I left the commons area and headed back to my room.

Wow! I couldn't believe how God had just given me the words to speak. They had so easily flowed out of my mouth. It was simply amazing! My frustration over what had just happened melted away, and a sense of peace started to fill me. However, I returned to my room. There, I met the first of my many roommates to come. We introduced ourselves and briefly shared minimal information and commonalities that had brought us to CHOICES. Our conversation ended as she shared the importance of adhering to all their guidelines. She emphasized that, although some were strict, they were all intended to keep us safe from harm.

Thoughts flowed through my mind as I readied for bed. They were all focused on what had happened and what I had experienced over the past months. God truly had been with me every minute. He'd led, guided, directed, and taken care of me through it all. I couldn't have done all that needed to be done all by myself. God had brought so many people into my life who were more than willing to help and support me in my times of trouble. I saw the hand of God at work within it all.

That night, I lay silently in my bed praising God for being my Savior, rescuer, refuge, comforter, and strength. Many thanks were also given to Him for providing me with this wonderful, safe place, my new "home away from home" known as CHOICES. I fell asleep saying much the same prayer that David did, saying, "You have given me greater joy…In peace, I will lie down and sleep, for you alone, O Lord, will keep me safe" (Psalm 4:7–8, NLT).

Words of Wisdom: *God tells us in His Word that we will have troubles in life. However, He also tells us in Romans 8:28 that "He works all things for the good of those who love Him and are called to His purpose." Thus, as Christians, it's safe to say that God will never waste our pains, problems, and troubles, for there is a purpose behind them all. Therefore, when you, again and again, find yourself praying, "Lord, get me out of this and/or turn this thing around," pause and consider these things:*

- *Maybe He's trying to show you that making your own choices is an extremely valuable and important gift He's given you. The choices you make today, whether good or bad, will determine your future tomorrow. He may be teaching you, in a hard way, that there are great benefits in making right choices so you avoid experiencing the drastic "should-ah, could-ah, would-ahs" of life.*

- *Maybe He's working on "turning you around." Life's trials and troubles are His classrooms designed to strengthen your faith and trust in Him. He's a great teacher and is most likely trying to teach you something about yourselves that first needs to change before He turns "that" thing around.*
- *And once you've joyfully exited His classroom having learned your lessons, you'll also start asking Him to help you make the right choices and strengthen your commitment to trust Him in all things…no matter what!*

There is always a purpose behind what and how things happen in life. Nothing is a coincidence or happens by chance. "Something" or someone has made it happen. Look deep into what, how, and why it happened. There is a purpose behind it all. Search for the purpose, and you will find God's hand working as He works through others within your life.

I woke up the next morning having slept peacefully and without fear for the first time in months. The feeling of being safe and secure filled me as I nestled in my new safe place. I was ready to start living my new life.

For the sake of not knowing what to expect after my escape, I had scheduled the remainder of the week off from work. Therefore, an extended long weekend awaited, and it allowed me the opportunity to adjust to my new environment. Oh, and it did prove to be an adjustment. Many timeframes and rules needed to be followed and adhered to. Many different lifestyles, attitudes, and outlooks on life abounded. Many of the women were unemployed or had lost their jobs because of the need to escape from their abusers. However, there was a common woven thread that tightly bound us all together. We were all victims of abuse.

After breakfast, I obtained directions and walked to the location where my car, for the time being, had to remain safely parked. The CHOICES staff member had spoken the truth about how far it was from my safe refuge. It was anything but close to it. However, the long walk to and from my car, which would soon become almost a daily trek, gave me a peaceful time to be with God. I was safe and, unlike some of the women, I still had my job, could drive to work, and continue paying my bills. The Lord was with me, and I thanked Him daily for loving and taking care of me.

Ya wanna talk about the Lord taking care of me? Here's a prime example that followed my return to CHOICES that morning. That afternoon, I overheard a fellow CHOICES tenant say that she was going to get her car and go to a post office. She had to get a P.O. Box and submit a forwarding address request as soon as possible.

Oh my gosh! I had overlooked doing this during the preparation for my escape. Keep in mind, there was no such thing as an online bill notice or electronic bill pay system at the time. Every bill was delivered by mail, and payment was made either in person or sent by mail.

For safety's sake, I couldn't go back to my townhouse daily to retrieve my mail, nor would I even think of asking Jo or Ken to do so. Immediately, I asked the lady if I could go with her, and she readily agreed. And even though it would periodically prove to be another long walk, I praised God and thanked her as we traveled to and from the Post Office.

Another of God's blessings came the very next morning as He introduced Delois into my life. She, along with her eleven-month-old and seven-year-old daughters, had boarded a Greyhound bus the night before, leaving behind everything they had to escape from her husband, their abuser.

My heart dropped when I first saw her. Her nose was broken, and both of her eyes were severely bruised and extremely swollen.

However, she still had a smile on her face. I soon found out why as she unapologetically praised God for getting them away from their abuser and safely to CHOICES.

I had not heard the name of God mentioned since arriving at CHOICES. Well, that is, except for when someone used His name in vain. Therefore, I had asked the Lord to help me identify a like-minded Christian believer within the group of ladies because I needed one. And there she was, standing in front of me. Hearing Delois praising God lifted my spirit. I had to get to know her!

We bonded almost immediately and mutually agreed that God had connected us on purpose and with a purpose. We were there for each other when needed and held daily private devotional time together with God.

Many of our discussions centered around two things. The first was the importance of making the right choices in life, and as we moved forward in our lives, to ask God to help us do so. The second topic was more of an agreement than a discussion. That agreement had everything to do with our present safe refuge, CHOICES. It had not been named that by accident. Our lives depend upon and are determined by the choices we make.

All the time we spent together proved to us the truth Jesus spoke when He said, "For where two or three gather in my name, there am I with them," Matthew 18:20. Our trust in God became stronger. Our friendship grew over the following weeks.

Many things happened during the eight weeks I spent living in my safe refuge. Thanks to God, Rose, Mark, and the understanding leadership of the Chamber and at CHOICES, I successfully and without a hitch continued to meet all the responsibilities of my job and the requirements of being a resident within my refuge. But putting that all aside for now, here are the four things that I vividly remember happening during those weeks.

Memory #1: "My Jesus Money"

Growing concern for my financial well-being had become a major concern. The debt I had to pay off due to the Payday loans Doug had previously obtained was outrageous. Plus, I had no idea how he was presently paying for his living expenses. Therefore, I had to play it safe and cut my expenses. The Chamber reimbursed much of the expenses I incurred while doing my job. However, they did not pay for daily parking garage expenses. Therefore, and for the time being, I determined I could no longer afford daily downtown parking.

The Chamber's approval was obtained for me to park in their free private parking lot located behind their offices. This lot was specifically designated for the use of the Chamber's upper-echelon leadership. Therefore, approval to do so would only be granted on a justifiable and as-needed basis, such as evening workshops or when I had to load and take tons of "after-work" work home with me. I graciously accepted their willingness to help in any way possible, and that meant, more often than not, I'd be walking to and from work, which I did.

Let me tell you, the walk to and from work was thousands of times farther compared to the walk I had to take to get to the location of CHOICES daily mandated parking area for my car.

However, there's an old saying that advises what to do when life gets tough. It goes something like this: "When life gives you lemons, make lemonade." Get ready for the lemonade God gave me on the many days and miles of walking to and from work.

My daily routine of walking to and from work mandated walking through many miles of non-metered streets. However, God's blessed lemonade would start to flow when I finally came to the many miles of city streets where metered parking was available. Keep in mind that the meter technology of today did not exist at that time. To pay for parking, you had to feed the meter and put coins into it.

The first time I took the trek to and from work, I couldn't believe how many quarters, dimes, and nickels lay on the sidewalk at the base of the meters. People simply did not bend over to retrieve their dropped coins. Well, I did! I picked up every coin on my way to and from work. Each time I did, I thanked God for blessing me and meeting every one of my needs down to the last penny and told Him how much I loved Him. Each coin was a sign and a blessing from God.

Every day, upon returning to CHOICES, the coins were securely put into a jar and kept under my bed in my locked suitcase. I called these coins my "Jesus money." They were my blessings from Him. I only used the money in times of dire need. My mom always loved to sing the song "Count Your Blessings." However, I never counted these coins of blessings. I just wanted to see them grow and fill the jar. And soon, I needed a larger jar!

Before I move on to "Memory #2," let me add that to this very day, everyone who knows me knows I still pick up every coin, no matter where they may lie. Everyone also knows the reason why I do. As a matter of fact, years later, when I went to meet with a client, a sign was posted on her office door. It advised me to enter and follow the trail. As I did, a steady trail of coins led me directly to her office. I bent over and picked up every last one of them! When I got to her office, she looked up at me and joyfully said, "Well, praise God. You are surely blessed and have found your way to me!"

I still call each coin my "Jesus money" and verbally give Him praise for each blessed one of them. I very seldom use this money, but at the end of the year, I now give it all back to God. Why? Because He loves me and has proven that "My God will meet all your needs according to the riches of his glory in Christ Jesus," (Philippians 4:19). And throughout all my years, no matter what that "need" may have been, He has always taken care of every one of them "down to the last penny."

Memory #2: Forgiveness

From day one at CHOICES, thoughts of Doug would anger me. Anger and hatred were the only mindsets that filled me when thinking of him. My anger and hatred applied to him as a person, and all that he had done to me. I seriously disliked him with great passion—that's my euphemism for the word *hate.*

Many hours were spent alone in my room or outside as I silently spent time with God and delved into His Word. As I did, I would also fervently pray that God would get Doug out of my life and help me wipe out every thought of him from my mind. Several weeks passed, and nothing was happening. The hateful thoughts prevailed because, as far as I knew, Doug was still a threat to my life and living in my home.

However, one day, as I sat reading my Bible and praying my standard "Get him out of my life" prayer, I heard from God. I had just read Matthew 5:44 (NLT), which says, "But I tell you, love your enemies and pray for those who persecute you." I automatically slammed my Bible shut and almost yelled, "What! Are you kidding me? You want me to love and pray for him?" As I calmed down, God's quiet reply was, *Yes, I love him, and so should you. You pray for yourself, so you should also pray for him. Give him over to Me along with all the troubles he's brought upon you.*

Now I must admit that, even though I believe that we should be "doers" of the Word and not "hearers" only, many minutes passed before I gave in and said, "Okay, Lord, here he is. I will commit to praying for him daily and giving him over to you. However, I'm going to find it hard to love him in the least little bit. He's hurt me so badly. And with that, I started praying for him daily. It was a short, simple, and somewhat cold daily prayer, of "Lord, here he is. Do what you will with him. Amen." And after every "amen," my mind would sneer and think, *Hey, at least I'm praying for him, God!*

Days later, God proved that He wasn't done with me yet. I was reading a devotional that focused on Colossians 3:12-13 (NLT), which says, "Since God chose you to be the holy people he loves, you must clothe yourselves with tenderhearted mercy, kindness, humility, gentleness, and patience. Make allowance for each other's faults." Now, even though there was more to the verse, I immediately stopped. That last statement hit my heart. I had to read it again.

As I, once again, read, "Make allowances for each other's faults," tears welled up in my eyes, and a tenderhearted, merciful prayer came out of my mouth asking God to forgive me for holding onto such a bitter and hateful attitude towards Doug. I remembered that his faults, which had hurt me so badly, hadn't come upon him willingly. They had started at the age of nine when his father slammed an axe into Doug's head. This act caused major brain damage and created a difficult life ahead of him. At that very moment, my prayers for Doug started to change. They would become clothed with all the characteristics noted in Colossians 3.

When my prayer ended, I returned to read the last sentence in Colossians 3:13. Here's what it said, "Make allowance for each other's faults, and forgive anyone who offends you. Remember, the Lord forgave you, so you must forgive others" (NLT). I stopped abruptly once again and said, "Oh my Gosh, Lord, now you want me to do what?! Forgive him? Are you kidding? I'm supposed to love him, pray for him, and now forgive him? Lord, You are really pushing the envelope here! He's hurt me so badly. I don't know if I want to, if I can, or even how to do it if I wanted to."

I returned to the Scripture passage and read the final part of the sentence and received the beginnings of "the how and why" of forgiving as I read, "Remember, the Lord forgave you, so you must forgive others." Please note this final statement starts with "remember" and ends with "must forgive" and not "should forgive." I must forgive!

Immediate prayers were shot up to God, asking Him to help me in my attempts to love, pray for, and especially forgive Doug. I knew I couldn't do it all by myself. I needed God's help to make it happen, and over the following days, He did exactly that. God provided me with many Scriptures and devotionals that guided my understanding and strengthened my efforts to sincerely do all three things.

My prayer for compassionate forgiveness to the Lord came one night as I sat outside in the quiet evening. Granted, it wasn't easy, but it was filled with a caring concern for Doug that I couldn't understand or explain.

I remember my sincere prayer went something like this: "Lord, I truly forgive Doug for the wrongs he's done against me and for the pain he has caused me. God, I forgive him because You've forgiven me of all my wrongdoings. Please lead, guide, direct, love, and protect him as You have done for me. Transform his life and bless him as You have done for me. Here he is, Lord. I lift him up to You. It's in your name, I pray. Amen."

As I said, "amen," it felt as though the weight of the world had been taken off my shoulders. A feeling of actually being set free came over me. It was then that I realized I had been living in a state of imprisonment, trapped by my own faults, hatred, and anger. Yet now I was set free from them.

My prisons had been created because of the choices I had made. I had created both of them. The first prison was the physical, emotional, and financially abusive relationship that all began because of the bad choices I had made months before in Arkansas. The second prison was built atop the first. Its prison bars had been strong like iron and formed by my choice not to let go of the bitter, hatefully resentful, and angry thoughts that filled my mind every time I thought of Doug. I had now forgiven him. And in so doing, I let go of all the thoughts that imprisoned me. It felt so good! I was set free and believed God would soon release and free me completely from the first.

> ***Words of Wisdom:*** *Loving, praying for, and forgiving those who have sinned against you, in any way, is a very important yet challenging task. To meet this threefold challenge, you must follow the standards that the Lord has set. Therefore, remember these things:*
>
> ***Love:***
>
> - *God is love. He loves you more than anyone on earth does or ever could. He created you to have someone to*

lovingly take care of, and His desire is for you to honor and love Him in return. But from the very beginning, mankind messed up, and sin entered the world. "But God showed his great love for us by sending Christ to die for us while we were still sinners" (Romans 5:8, NLT). Jesus even expressed His love and willingness to die for your sins by saying in John 15:13 (NLT), "There is no greater love than to lay down one's life for one's friends." And He did! He died for the atonement of your sins. You can now claim the promise made to us in Romans 8 that nothing will be able to separate you from God's love that is in Christ Jesus.

So, when it comes to loving others, realize Romans 3:23 (NLT) speaks the truth when it says, "For everyone has sinned; we all fall short of God's glorious standard." Therefore, strive to live up to God's standards. Love the ones you love to love and love your enemies as well.

Pray:

- *Jesus prayed for His people. He's even praying for you now. Through His Holy Spirit, the Lord is praying for you. He even prays for you when you don't even know what to pray for. Regardless of the circumstances, continue to pray for your enemies. James 5:16 says, "The earnest prayer of a righteous person has great power and produces wonderful results" (NLT).*

Forgive:

- *According to God's standards, forgiveness is a must. God, through His Son, Jesus Christ, has and will forgive ALL your sins, mess-ups, and failures. Jesus died on an old, rugged cross for the total atonement for them. However, when it comes to forgiving, never forget the "Must Factor!" Matthew 6:14–15 says, "For if you forgive other people when they sin against you, your heavenly Father will also forgive you. But if you do not forgive others their sins, your Father will not forgive your sins." Therefore, forgive those who have, in any way, sinned against you. When you do, God will continue to forgive you. He guarantees it and will bring peace to your soul and free your spirit. You'll be set free, healed, and grow when you let go!*

God has set the standards, and Jesus set the example of following them to the 'T'.

Follow Jesus's lead. Love, pray for, and forgive, just like He did. God will never ask—you to do something that His Son hasn't already done.

Memory # 3 : Miracle Within an Unexpected Call

The month of May was only days away, and May 3rd would mark the beginning of my eighth week living at CHOICES. Keeping its location undisclosed was not a problem, but I desperately missed seeing my family. Office interactions with coworkers continued. Weekly calls to or from Jo kept her assured that all was okay with me and gave me the opportunity to ask her if there were still signs of Doug living in the townhouse. Her answer to that question was always, "Yes." After each of these calls, I'd pray, "Lord, get him out of my life and out of my home! I can't safely go home and start a new life until he's gone and nowhere near my family or me.

May 3rd came, and so did an office call from my CHOICES case manager. She wanted to meet with me upon my return to CHOICES that evening. During our meeting, she expressed concern that I was still a resident and asked what plan of action I had to move forward in my life.

God had to have given me the words to answer her question. I explained that escaping my mentally and emotionally ill abuser was not the only reason I was still there. It was also to prevent, as the psychologist had stated, "a murder-suicide from happening." And Doug, my abuser, was still living in my home. Therefore, for fear of not only my own life but also my family's lives, I couldn't even think of safely going home to retrieve any of my belongings or moving anywhere.

However, she assured me that, no matter what, a clearer plan to move forward had to be developed. And, in her opinion, that plan should include moving out of the townhouse and into a place in a different town.

I was in tears by the end of our meeting and praying for God to grant me grace and mercy. And that He did. As I left her office, the case manager put her arm around my shoulder, assuring me she understood. She also committed to exploring ways to extend my stay at CHOICES until the end of the month, with the goal of providing her with a plan of action that would move me forward soon. God's grace and mercy flooded over me as I left her office.

My prayers that night covered the following:

- Thanking God for always taking care of me.
- Claiming, in the name of Jesus, that God would work within my circumstances, and I'd be granted an extended stay at CHOICES.
- He'd help me develop a plan.
- Help me find an affordable place to live, and once found, provide a safe way to move all my stuff out of the townhouse into a new place.

- I shared my fears that even having a good plan to live in a different place and town, Doug would still be in my life and able to find and cause me harm or kill me.
- My prayers ended by saying, "I can't do this all by myself. I'm begging You. Help me, Lord. Keep me safe. Here it is, Lord, and here am I. Lead, guide, and direct every decision and every step. Lord, I need You. I'm desperate."

With those prayer requests in mind, I started penciling a feeble plan that I only hoped would temporarily appease my case manager.

However, everything would change the very next morning. Jo had called the office and left me a message that simply stated, "Call me! I have some exciting news!" I immediately called her.

Her news was fabulous!

Ken had bought a Greyhound bus ticket to Arkansas and given it to Doug. As he handed him the ticket, Ken told him it was his ticket home to Arkansas and that he shouldn't plan to ever return to Ohio. Doug had willingly accepted the ticket, and Ken would be taking him to the bus station. Doug would be gone from my life within days! When that day came, I received another message from Jo. It was only two words that joyfully advised, "He's gone!"

I immediately called her back. Pure joy and many praises to God poured out of our mouths throughout our conversation. My greatest shared praise to God was for how He had worked through it all. He had worked through Ken, the man who used to greatly dislike me for emotionally hurting his wife in the past. Ken had first provided Doug with trusted counsel. Next, he had arranged a much-needed conversation with a psychologist for me. And now God had worked through him to become and serve as my rescuer, who would send my abuser away and never return.

Jo's reply to all of this was not only to join me in my praises but to add, "Nancy, the operable term in all you just said about Ken was 'used to.' Ken has seen and experienced how you are changing, and we are both praising God for that." As our call ended, she assured me that they both were there for me. We then agreed to meet the following night to jointly develop a plan that would move my life forward.

As I hung up the phone, I felt held within the loving arms of God. The doors of Heaven had been opened. Tons of love and blessings were being poured over me. My family and I would now be safe. My next steps would soon be developing a plan of action to present to the case manager at CHOICES.

Three major thoughts permeated my thoughts as I fell asleep that night.

- The first focused on the fact that I hadn't done anything to finally and successfully get Doug out of my life. God, working through others, had made it all happen. And with that thought came my humble prayer saying, "Lord, You've proven, time and time again, to me that You make things happen when I can't. God, You are God and I am not. Please forgive me for ever thinking that I was.

- Then, I realized that even though I had prayed, "God, get Doug out of my life," God had to first get me out of Doug's life to make it all happen.
- Many heartfelt thanks flowed up to God for taking care of me when I didn't even know He was. He had orchestrated it all, and now it was all coming to fruition. The Lord had heard my cry and answered my prayers.

Jo and I met as planned, and here's the "Moving Forward Plan of Action" presented to the CHOICES case manager the very next day:

- Move out of CHOICES by the end of the week and into the second-floor living area and guest bedroom of Jo and Ken's former home. Since Jo still operated her business out of their former home, all utilities and kitchen areas were operable and in use.
- All use of my living area would be provided at no charge and available to me until I secured a place of my own.
- Immediately, begin looking for an affordable place to rent

in a different town. Preferably close to or within the same town where Jo and Ken lived.

- May's townhouse rent had already been paid. Therefore, this would give me time to clean the townhouse and pack my belongings to be moved either into a storage unit or my new home.
- The townhouse's month-to-month lease agreement would be canceled effective June 1st.
- May 31st would be my goal date to secure a new home of my own. However, if that was not accomplished, I could continue to live in Jo and Ken's former home, at no charge, until a home of my own was secured.

The case manager was ecstatic. She couldn't believe how I had gone from basically no plan to the one that had just been presented to her. Giving God all the glory, I shared all that had happened since our last meeting. We were both praising God as I left her office.

Memory # 4: Heartfelt Goodbyes

Word that I was leaving started to flow through the resident grapevine. All were happy for me. However, there were two ladies who, although happy for me, were also deeply saddened by the news.

The first one was the last of my many roommates. She, although only in her mid-twenties, had lived a hard, abused life. We had shared several nights talking about her past abusive experiences and how unloved she felt. In those moments, God gave me the words of support and encouragement to share with her. He also gave me multiple times to tell her how much God loved her more than anyone on earth could. There were many other times we would simply sit outside in silence, doing whatever. But she always knew I was there for her if she needed me.

The night after the news of my departure hit the resident grapevine, I had a workshop to conduct and arrived back at CHOICES much later than usual. There were not many women in the commons area, so I decided to go straight to my room. My young roommate was sitting on her bed, sobbing and crying her eyes out. Immediately, I went to her and asked if she was okay.

I will never forget her reply as she looked up at me with tears flowing down her face. Her mournful eyes met mine as she said, "No, I'm not okay. I don't want you to leave. Please don't leave me."

Me being me, I went over, sat on her bed, put my arm around her shoulder, and said, "Oh, honey, it'll be okay."

She abruptly looked back up at me and said, "Oh no, it won't. I don't want you to leave. You have shown me so much heartfelt love in the past weeks. You've shown me that you do care about me. You've given me the kind of caring love I've never had. You've been my spiritual support and caring friend even in our quiet times. Now, I'll be all alone. I doubt if anyone will care about me like you have. To me, you've been the perfect example of love. You've been the mom I always wanted but never had."

That statement hit my heart hard and made it ache for her. Squeezing her shoulder, I said, Oh, honey, I'm by no means perfect. I just try my best to be who God wants me to be. Sometimes I succeed, but a lot of times I fail. And, as far as you being alone and unloved, that's totally untrue. You'll never be alone. God will always be with you and never abandon or forsake you. He'll be with you and loving you every day, every step of the way. And here's the cool thing about His love. It's unconditional. God loves you just the way you are. He only wants the best for you. Matter of fact, He loves you more than any person ever will or ever could.

We sat there quietly with my arm around her shoulder for quite a while.

Gently squeezing her shoulder one last time, she looked up at me with puffy, tear-filled eyes and said, "See, that's what I'm talking about. Nancy, your love and faith in God shout in your silence." Her statement humbled me greatly, as I thanked God for beginning His transformative work within me.

That night, silent prayers were lifted to God on her behalf. I praised Him for being who He was in my life and asked Him to be the same within her life. I asked the Lord to continue helping her, as well as me, to grow into who He had planned and designed for both of us to become.

Delois, my wonderful sister in Christ, was the second to express her mixed feelings of happiness and sadness. We had become close friends in the past weeks and had served as each other's support base and Bible study partners. I considered this time our own spiritual and Christ-centered small group gathering, as Matthew 18:20 (NLT) says, "For where two or three gather in my name, there am I with them." And over the weeks, He proved He was always with us. We shared many of our life experiences, how God had taken care of us, and how He miraculously helped us get through them all. We both agreed on two things. First, we had both grown in our faith thanks to the time we'd spent together. And secondly, we would seriously miss each other and our daily companionship and spiritual support.

Words of Wisdom: *Never overlook or miss the opportunity to share and show the love of God with others. In all you do and say, let the love of God shine through you. Plant the "Good News" seed into someone's life. Then nurture it. You won't* *regret your efforts, for God will not only strengthen their faith, but yours as well.*

Growing in God while fighting the devil is difficult to do alone. You can't successfully do it all by yourself. Matter of fact, God never intended you to do it all by yourself. Ecclesiastes 4:9–10 (NLT) tells us that," Two people are better off than one, for they can help each other succeed. If one person falls, the other can reach out and help. But someone who falls alone is in real trouble." You need a trusted, like-minded Christian friend who will come alongside you, provide words of encouragement, challenge you, help strengthen your efforts, and pick you up when you fall. A Christ-centered support group of believers is also most beneficial because Ecclesiastes 4:12 (NLT) says, "A person standing alone can be attacked and defeated, but two can stand back-to-back and conquer. Three are even better, for a triple-braided cord is not easily broken."

If you don't have these essential growth and support elements in your life, diligently seek them out. You need them! If you do have them, praise God for them by name. Then, connect with them and express your gratitude for their presence in your life. If you know someone who needs either of these support essentials, reach out to them. Become that Christ-centered friend and support them. Invite them into your life and support group.

Then humbly let the love of God shine through you as you reinforce their growth in God.

My last night at CHOICES was spent with the two most important people in my life at that time. Delois and the Lord. One, I would be leaving behind. The other, I would never leave behind. God would always be with me.

Dinner was spent with Delois and her family. I loved them all. After the kids had gone to their room, Delois and I held our last "small group get-together." The Lord was, once again, definitely there with us. Our entire time was spent praising God for CHOICES and discussing how important it is to make the right God-centered choices in our future. God had brought us both to CHOICES to emphasize the fact that safely and happily living life on earth is dependent upon the choices we make.

Words of Wisdom: *The choices we make in life direct the trajectory of our lives. One of the greatest gifts God gave us as human beings was the ability to make our own choices. He doesn't force us to do anything. We have the choice to do what is right or what we know is wrong. Making the right choice, although sometimes hard, tends to improve our lives. Making* *the wrong choice tends to be easier, but in the long run, our lives become harder, filled with trouble, turmoil, and "Should-ah, Could-ah, Would-ah" moments. That's when God steps in and turns our wrong choices into great yet hard learning lessons. Therefore, let us learn not only from our good choices but also from the bad choices that we make. Then apply what we've learned in our lives, so the chances of winning increase and the hard lessons decrease. However, remember this: We are the ones who choose and decide to either win or continue learning . . . the hard way.*

Delois confirmed that fact by reiterating some of the bad choices we'd both made. However, she then emphasized the truth held in Proverbs 20:30 (GNT), which states, "Sometimes it takes a painful experience to make us change our ways." Oh, and change was exactly what we both wanted.

I thought Delois was done. But praise God, she wasn't. She asked me to look up Psalm 119:71 and read it aloud because she had one last thing to add, confirming all we had discussed and shared. I opened my Bible and read aloud Psalm 119:71 (NLT), which states, "My suffering was good for me, for it taught me to pay attention to your decrees."

Oh my gosh! It truly had been good for me! I realized that my faith in God had grown stronger during this terrifying, tumultuous, and painful time in my life. All I could do was praise God for He had taught me well, and I had learned.

This led to Delois saying, "Nancy, you know they say God never wastes a pain. He puts His purpose within it while He helps us get through it." Her statement led to even more sharing. Each of us shared examples of how God had been with us, taken care of us, and what He had taught us through it all.

Our get-together ended as we prayed, asking God to help us daily apply what He had taught us because we never again wanted to go through what we had just been through. We asked for His wisdom and guidance in making better choices. And as we both said, "Amen," we committed to keeping Him at the center of our lives and to striving every day to pay attention to His commands.

Delois and I agreed on one last thing as we walked to our rooms. We needed each other. Therefore, no matter what our futures held, we would stay connected and continue serving as spiritual growth support to and for each other. And that we did.

Words of Wisdom: *Life is a classroom. Its lesson plans are troubled problems. Respond to them in the right way.*

Don't ask God why they're happening. Instead, ask Him, "What are you trying to teach me through this? Learn from His instruction and then apply what you've learned. Sure, it's going to be painful, but remember, your body didn't grow from infancy to adulthood without growing pains. The same principle applies to growing in life. Painful problems are the high cost of growth. However, realize that your greatest growth in life doesn't happen on life's mountain tops. It happens in its valleys. Take just a moment right now, get online, and go to https://bit.ly/4atGplb. It's an awesome poem written by Jane Eggleston entitled "It's in the Valleys that I Grow." Listen to its music as you read and reflect on its words. You'll totally understand what I'm talking about. With this realization, you'll be more than able to proclaim Romans 5:3–4 (TLB), which states, "We can rejoice, too, when we run into problems and trials, for we know that they are good for us. They help us learn to be patient. And patience develops strength of character in us and helps us trust God more each time we use it." And always remember, the choices you have made in the past have created your past. However, the choices you make now, whether good or bad, will determine your future.

The Lord was alive within me as I returned to my room for the last time. A note from my roomie awaited me when I entered. She would not be returning to CHOICES until curfew time and promised to be quiet when she came in. Therefore, the night of packing and preparing to leave in the morning became my own special quiet time of praise and prayer with God.

I turned on the radio. Christian contemporary music filled the room, and I joyfully sang right along with it as I packed. Almost every song filled my heart with peace and assurance that the Lord was with me. My mind praised Him for how He had guided, directed, protected, and loved me throughout my entire life, especially the past few months. And now, I was moving forward in my life with Him by my side.

As I finished packing, my quiet prayer time began. All prayers were focused on asking God for His forgiveness and acknowledging my need for Him. I asked God to help me keep Him as the central focus of my life. I asked that He strengthen my efforts to renew my mind. I wanted to model Jesus more and more each day in everything I did and said.

My quiet prayer time ended as I shared with Him the most important thing I wanted. I bowed my head and, from my heart, I said, "Lord, I want to trust You more. In all I do, say, and within every choice I make, I, first and foremost, want to look to you first.

I want to trust You in everything. In any and every circumstance or situation. 'No matter what,' I want to trust You. You've proven to me time and time again that you are more than worthy of my trust. Therefore, I want to trust You more. You've been my great, understanding, and loving teacher throughout my life. Here I am, Lord, teach me how to grow to trust You, 'No Matter What' the case may be."

I hopped into bed, closed my eyes, and prayed for a peaceful, rejuvenating night's sleep. However, initially, my mind refused to allow that to happen due to two exciting thoughts that permeated through it. First, I knew God had heard my prayers and would answer them. The other reason was that my brain wouldn't stop shouting, *Tomorrow's the day! I'll finally be moving forward in my life. I'll be free! Free at last!*

My mind finally settled down as my thoughts drifted to my favorite Bible verse. Its words flowed through my mind. "Trust in the Lord with all your heart and lean not on your own understanding; In all your ways acknowledge Him, and He shall direct your paths" (Proverbs 3:5–6, NKJV).

Those words from God have always soothed my soul, and to this very day, I still thank Him for them. My thoughts settled down. Once again, I told Him that "No Matter What" my future brings,

I wanted to trust Him with all my heart. As I drifted off to sleep, I heard a small, quiet voice within me say,

Be still and know that I am God.

Get ready!

I'm about to do a New Thing!

~ 12~
FREE AT LAST

The day of my deliverance began early the next morning. The chore of getting dressed for the day was a piece of cake since everything else had been packed and was ready to go. Once dressed, I walked the long distance to where my car had to be parked while living at CHOICES. However, this time I didn't mind the walk at all. It was a beautiful sunny morning. The new life, beauty, and fragrances of spring were all around me. It made the "last time trek" to my car a grand celebration to God for taking care of me and for the new life that was awaiting me.

Upon returning to CHOICES, all my things were loaded into the car. The breakfast hour was spent with the closest friends I'd made while there. We all agreed that we'd greatly miss the camaraderie that we'd developed. But we also promised that, as time passed, we'd do our best to stay in touch.

Sad yet joyful goodbyes were shared as I signed out of CHOICES for the last time and exited what had been my safe refuge. Overwhelming joy filled my spirit as I hopped into my car and yelled, "I'm free! Free at last!" And declared to the Lord as I drove away, "I'm moving forward into whatever You have in store for me."

When I arrived at Jo's, she joyfully came running out to greet me, and many loving hugs were shared. She took me on a guided tour of their former home, now renovated into a business site, and led me up to my slightly renovated temporary second-floor home. It was beautifully done, yet still felt like home.

As we unloaded the car into my new temporary home, she asked how traffic was. I told her it had been okay. However, it had been over eight weeks since I had driven my car any distance. Therefore, the drive had seemed unusual, and I felt as though it had taken forever to get there. Jo laughed and reminded me that I used to define that very same route as "You'll get there in a whipstitch." We both laughed and agreed that my feelings were probably based on my strong desire to just get there and that my "whipstitch" route definition would soon return.

She then invited me to join Ken and her for dinner. But I declined, stating that I had unpacking to do and just wanted to use the evening to relax and enjoy settling into my new temporary abode. With that said, she took me to their new kitchen area, which they had moved to the basement, showed me all the food available, and told me to help myself. I gave her a big smile and a thumbs-up on that.

We went back upstairs, and as we did, she told me how glad she was to have me staying in their newly renovated business home while I searched for one of my own. She then gave me all the keys and passcodes necessary to live there securely, hugged me, said that she'd call me later, and said goodbye.

As she drove away, the quietness of my environment fell around me. It sounded wonderful. I stood there in silence, thanking God for how He had orchestrated it all. He had delivered me. He had kept me safe, met all my needs, driven out every ounce of fear I had held, and wiped away every one of my worries. I was free of them all. My family and I were safe once again.

Those thoughts were briefly followed by a consideration of whether to visit the townhouse. However, I quickly decided not to worry about it. It could wait until tomorrow. And as I quoted Matthew 6:34, which states, "Do not worry about tomorrow, for tomorrow will worry about itself. Each day has enough trouble of its own." I also added, much like Scarlet O'Hara did in Gone with the Wind, "After all, tomorrow is another day."

I spent the rest of the day unpacking, settling into my new temporary home, and finding something to wear to tomorrow's Sunday church service.

The thought of attending church was exhilarating and energizing. It had been months since I had been able to even think about going to church without fear of being ridiculed or abused. I wanted to go to church on Sunday. I had to find something to wear. The townhouse could wait till after church tomorrow. That night, as I went to bed, I once again praised God for how He had gone before me, set me free by working through Jo and Ken, and for all He and they had and were doing for me.

Sunday morning came, and so did the joy of attending church again. The small church I had previously been attending was within walking distance of Jo and Ken's. The walk to church was liberating, and the thought of simply attending the service was exhilarating.

Everyone was glad to see me. The service was fabulous. I remember thinking, *God, you even knew I was going to be here today. The message was perfect. It was as if you were speaking directly to me through the pastor's words.*

After the service, two of my closest friends came up to me to joyfully welcome me back. They said that they had been praying for me because neither of them could get in touch with me. They were concerned and had been wondering what had happened to me and where I'd been.

They were shocked as I shared, without going into any detail, what had happened over the past months. However, they were overjoyed to hear that I was now safe and had begun a new life. Wonderful hugs were shared, and as I left, they promised to keep me in their prayers.

Thoughts of my last night at CHOICES filled my mind as I walked back to the house. The quiet words I had heard from God as I fell asleep that night repeated within me. "Be still and know that I am God. Get ready! I'm about to do a New Thing!"

I knew God had put those words in my mind because they were somewhere in the Bible. So as soon as I got home, I started searching the concordance of my NLT Bible and found them in Isaiah 43.

The first part of the chapter was filled with the Lord telling the Israelites how and what He had done to deliver them from Egypt. However, smack dab in the middle of the chapter (verses 18–19), there it was! "But forget all that—it is nothing compared to what I am going to do. For I am about to do something new. See, I have already begun! Do you not see it? I will make a pathway through the wilderness. I will create rivers in the dry wasteland."

My spirit was jumping for joy. That "new thing" was my new life that had just begun. All I wanted to do and did all day long was quietly spend my time basking in my thoughts on the remarkable things He had done to ignite this new beginning and thanking Him for it all. The entire day was spent with all my thoughts, praise, and prayers focused on thanking Him for taking care of me throughout my life. He made it all happen and never failed to use it all for my good. I humbly thanked Him for showering me with His glorious grace, mercy, and love.

However, at some point in the day, thoughts of going to the townhouse crossed my mind. But, without hesitation, I once again told myself, "Tomorrow is another day," and decided to put it off until Monday. At that moment, I wanted nothing to do with even thinking or dealing with the past months of my life. It could wait until tomorrow.

Words of Wisdom: *It's true! Nowhere in the Bible did God ever promise us a perfect, carefree, and trouble-free life here on earth. In fact, as John 16:33 states, Jesus told his disciples that they would have troubles in this world. Then James alludes to this fact in his letter to first-century believers when he said, "Blessed is the one who perseveres under trial because, having stood the test, that person will receive the crown of life that the lord has promised to those who love him" (James 1:12).*

When it comes to the troubles and trials you face in life, let me encourage you to do one important thing. View them as though you have entered God's training room designed to help you become stronger and more like Jesus. If you do that, you can and will persevere and be blessed by them. Think back to a troubled time in your life. As you do, you might be able to identify how God refined you, developed your character, and increased your capacity to handle it all. Realize that God, the greatest trainer ever, works behind the scenes to strengthen all you do to get you through it all and be better and stronger than you were before.

If you are going through a difficult time right now, take James 1:12 to heart! You can stand firm, persevere, and have a promised reward awaiting you in heaven. Sure, rewards aren't promised here on earth but knowing one awaits you in heaven gives you hope and strength to endure the world trials and troubles that this world befalls you.

Whenever you are going through a difficult season of life, take time to focus on God's promises. He promised to always be with you. He will never leave you or abandon you. Step by step, He'll walk alongside you through it all. He will lead, guide, and direct you as He loves and protects you. And when you get through it, you and all that is you will be modeled and formed more like Jesus Christ.

Before you read on, take a moment and praise God for His unfailing faithfulness. Thank Him for leading, guiding, directing, loving, and protecting you at all times and in all things.

~ 13~
MOVING FORWARD

Tomorrow had turned into today. It was now Monday morning, and a busy day at work awaited me. While getting ready for work, I told myself that, no matter what, I could not put off going over to the townhouse after work. That was not an option. I had to go, whether I was ready for it or didn't feel like doing it.

The day at work was most challenging for some reason. Even though nothing seemed to have changed, nothing seemed to be going right. Therefore, when 5:00 p.m. came, I joyfully said, "Goodbye," and left it all behind me.

I kept my commitment to go to the townhouse. After a quick bite at Wendy's, I hopped into my car and headed for the townhouse. My mind held nothing but images of a damaged, wrecked, and disheveled home. Therefore, the entire drive was spent bracing myself for what might be awaiting me as I walked into what used to be my home.

I was amazed as I entered the townhouse. The place was not a total wreck. As a matter of fact, it seemed as if nothing major was missing or out of place. There were no holes punched into the walls, no unhinged doors gapping open, nor trash covering the floors. The entire place looked as though I had only been gone for a moment. Yet, when I began going through my personal belongings, I found that much was missing.

Anything of personal value, including all my jewelry, vintage record albums and CDs, my Arkansas Razorback winter jacket, and my hidden stash of over $200 "just-in-case" money, was gone. However, these missing things did not disturb me. Why wasn't I upset? The answer lay within my past. God had taught me some great lessons as a result of thieves breaking into my Texas home, stealing all my worldly possessions, and then burning my house down to hide the theft. Through that burglary, I learned:

- John 10:10a is true. No matter what type of thief you're talking about, they only come to steal, kill, and destroy.
- John 10:10b is also true, for it states, "I have come that they may have life, and have it to the full." The Lord was with me, kept me safe, and never failed to meet all my needs in all things at all times.
- Worldly possessions are just a bunch of *"stuff"* that you don't really need. It's all here one minute and gone the next.
- The true value in life is found through a loving relationship with God and His Son, Jesus Christ.
- Everything we have in life is a God-given gift to us.

Therefore, I considered my losses to be nothing. Instead, I saw them as blessings. To me, they became a sign of how Doug had managed to survive without a job and on his own. He had probably pawned most of the stuff and spent the "just-in-case" money to live on. However, I knew that there was no way Doug would have even thought of pawning the Razorback jacket. He was a big Razorback fan and loved the jacket as much as I did. I knew it was now in Arkansas, either hanging in his closet or keeping him warm, as it made him look "cool." And that was perfectly fine with me.

A peaceful, relieved feeling filled me after completing the quick inventory and confirming that the townhouse and everything in it were well intact. However, as I stood there looking around, a horrific realization hit me hard. I realized I still had a lot of stuff! And all that stuff had to be packed and moved out of the townhouse in less than three weeks. Plus, I was determined to leave the property cleaner and in better condition than when I moved in.

That thought was followed by one pleading yet brief verbal prayer, "Oh Lord, help me, please. I need help!" My prayer was immediately followed by grabbing my phone to start making help-me-please calls. But a knock on my front door stopped me in my tracks.

It was my landlord who lived in the townhouse adjacent to mine. The first thing he said as I opened the door was, "I've gotten your rent checks every month, but where've you been? I haven't seen you around."

I welcomed him in and told him it was a long story and that all was okay now. A concerned look crossed his face as he started to ask more questions, which I avoided answering in any detail. Although he had always been somewhat friendly, kind, and considerate, I didn't trust him in any sense of the word. In my opinion, he had only been that way because he just wanted me as his tenant and my rent money.

To intentionally stop him from asking more questions that I didn't want to answer, I looked at him and said, "I planned on telling you this next week, but since you're here, let me tell you what's happening in my life right now." I informed him that I was presently living somewhere else and looking for another place to live. I was there to begin preparations to move out by the end of the month, if not sooner. Therefore, he should consider my lease agreement canceled, null, and void on May 31st. I also requested that the final property walk-through be scheduled the day I vacated the property. I assured him that I would leave the property in as good or better condition than when I became his tenant. Therefore, I would also expect my security deposit to be fully refunded to me at that time as well.

He was shocked and tried to talk me out of moving. Nothing I said satisfied him. His kind words and concerned spirit vanished into thin air. He became argumentative and confrontational. I stood my ground and, without going into detail, told him I had to move, and assured him that the place would be left clean and ready for his next tenant. Nothing satisfied him. And as memories of dealing with Doug started to bleed back into my thoughts, my hand came up, and with its palm facing him, I energetically yelled, "Stop! This isn't doing either of us any good. I have to move, and I'll be out of here by May 31st." I thanked him for being my landlord and for his cooperation in the present matter at hand. He left in a huff, mumbling something under his breath. And that was the last time I saw him until the final walk-through occurred.

I stood there, somewhat frustrated and stunned. What shocked me about the whole thing was that his attitude and the words he'd just spoken had shown his true character. He was self-centered and had no compassion or care for my well-being. They had totally flipped from what they had been in the past and confirmed his true colors and my suspicion that he only wanted my rent money.

A strong resolve grew within me as I shut the door behind him. I was moving out and upward into my new life somewhere else. But a lot had to be accomplished in less than three weeks. Several moments later, the townhouse was securely locked, and I headed out to purchase moving supplies and hire people to help me move. There was nothing that was going to stop me.

Instead of returning to the townhouse that night, I went back to my temporary home at Jo's. The day had been challenging in every aspect. Work and this landlord experience had been enough for one day. By the end of the day, the car was loaded with moving boxes and supplies, and I knew that with a good night's sleep, I'd be ready to handle it all tomorrow. "After all, tomorrow is another day."

~ 14 ~
A NIGHT OF REVELATION AND RESOLVE

The Revelation

That night, while sitting in the peaceful environment of my bedroom, my thoughts flowed from one thing to another. However, they weren't focused on the events of the day but rather on the past months of my life with Doug.

Those months had definitely proved to be yet another hard lesson God had taught me regarding the choices I had made. And, once again, I thanked the Lord for never abandoning me, and for keeping His promise made to me when He provided me a way out of it (1 Corinthians 10:13). Through it all, He had lovingly taken care of me as I learned the errors of my ways.

However, as my mind rambled through the past months of living within an abusive relationship, every thought became a question of why.

I had always been a take-charge, in control, and independent person. I definitely hadn't been that person with Doug. Questions of why I did or didn't do this or that started to flood my mind. I didn't understand. Therefore, I asked God to help me identify and understand all the whys behind how I had handled myself and my past circumstances.

Dear Reader: *I'm sure you've been asking yourself some of the same why questions I asked myself that night. But before I share my list of whys with you. I want you to know two things.*

1. *No one truly knows how they will react to or within any given situation or circumstance until they are in it themselves. Therefore, some of my reasoning may seem illogical to you. However, every choice was rational to me at the time, even though I see the error of my thought process in hindsight.*
2. *Many of the answers to my "Why did I do what I did" questions were later validated in a research study conducted by The Institute for Family Studies. Their findings were published in 2016 in an article authored by Jason Whiting entitled "8 Reasons Why Women Stay in Abusive Relationships." All eight reasons were detailed in depth within the article and covered:*

- *Distorted Thoughts*
- *Damaged Self-Worth*
- *Fear*
- *Wanting to be a savior*

- *Children (I praise God this was not an issue in my case.)*
- *Family Expectations and Experiences*
- *Financial Constraints*
- *Isolation*

I had experienced many of these reasons during my abusive relationship with Doug.

Any insights taken from the Institute's study are stated in italics within the "why" answers I identified during my soul-searching efforts that night. If you are interested in taking note of their entire findings, please go online to https://bit.ly/4tzH5xW.

I truly believe the Lord guided my deep-dive soul-searching process that night. You'll see many of the Institute's findings woven into and throughout my reasons and responses. So, here's my list of questions and my soul-searching responses.

- Why didn't I call the police when he had surprisingly shown up at my front door and refused to leave?
    - Initially, I was in shock and scared when he showed up at my door. What could the police do? He hadn't hurt me. He just showed up unexpectedly and unwanted.

o Fear and confusion set in as I remembered the terror he showed during the last night I'd spent with him in Arkansas. ***Fear.*** *The threat of bodily and emotional harm is powerful, and abusers use this to control and keep women trapped.* Doug had certainly done this from day one.

o I thought, given time, I could help him find a job and another place to live, or leave and go back to Arkansas. ***Wanting to be a Savior:*** *Many women described a desire to help their abuser with the hopes of changing him or the situation.*

- Why did I allow him to stay?

o He had no money, car, or other place to go. He couldn't hold down a job due to his brain damage and emotional problems. He refused to leave because he couldn't afford to rent a place, nor could I. ***Financial Constraints:*** *Many referred to financial limitations.* And me being me, I couldn't heartlessly shove him out to the street. Therefore, ***Wanting to be a Savior*** came into play because of my *desire to help.* But, as time passed, every time the subject of his moving out was brought up, the powerful fear of being abused flared, became real, and I gave up trying because. I couldn't make him leave. ***Distorted Thoughts:*** *Being controlled and hurt is traumatizing. This leads to confusion and doubts. Perpetrators harass and accuse their victims, which wears them down and causes guilt and despair.*

  - I thought that I deserved all that was happening to me because of the guilt I felt for what I had done during my pre-Thanksgiving weekend in Arkansas. Therefore, I had brought it all upon myself and that was definitely a ***Distorted Thought.***

- Why did I feel obligated to pay his debt?
  - That's a good question since I was not a co-signer. I guess after being controlled, traumatized, hurt, and wrongly accused of many things so many times, distorted thoughts came into play once again. He had no income, but I did. I cared about him, didn't want him to get into trouble. Therefore, given my financial wherewithal and being pressured multiple times to cover his debt, I agreed to pay it off for him. Here again, it was the ***Wanting to be a Savior*** coming alive in me to save not only him from harm but myself as well. At the time, I didn't think this demand was abuse.

- Why did I wait so long to share what was going on in my life with family and close friends?
  - Simply put, I was guilt-ridden, ashamed, and embarrassed. I had been raised within a caring and loving Christian family. I wanted to keep it a secret from them to avoid ridicule and/or disappointing them, because I had failed them and gotten myself into this terrible mess. ***Damaged Self-Worth:*** *Many women felt beaten down and of no value, and*

related it to the emotional damage created as a result of the degrading treatment they experienced. The people with whom I worked also knew I was a Christian. I didn't want them to know what was going on in my private life for fear of being ridiculed, criticized, and becoming the office grapevine's ongoing hot topic. I had to protect my personal and professional reputation and worth from being damaged.

  - Doug had isolated me from all my friends and family. Outside human contact was totally forbidden except while I was at work. But even then, his multiple daily degrading calls caused my fearful frustrations to build. The detailed reports of whom I had talked to during the day, and then being belittled and wrongly accused of sleeping with every man I had mentioned, created additional fears and frustrations within me. My anxiety grew with each call and every interrogating workday report. ***Isolation:*** *A common tactic of manipulative partners is to separate their victim from family and friends. Sometimes this is physical, other times isolation is emotional.*
  - I thought I had to and could handle it all and save myself. This was my own attempt to hold onto my self-worth.

- Why did I put up with emotional, physical, and financial abuse for so long?
  - I truly believed that I had brought it all upon myself. Refer to ***Distorted Thoughts.***

- Fear! I was afraid of him and petrified of what he might do if I didn't do what he wanted, when and how he wanted me to do it. I also had this dreaded fear that if I left him, he'd somehow find me, and when he did, his terrible wrath would come barreling down upon me even worse. After all, the man was not stupid. He had developed a secret plan that got him from Arkansas to Ohio, and thanks to my stupid mistake of giving him my address, he showed up at my front door. If he had done it once, he could do it again. ***Fear:*** *Female victims of violence are much more likely than male victims to be terrorized and traumatized. Attempting to leave an abuser is dangerous. One woman felt* (as I did) *trapped because of her husband's "threats of hunting me down and harming all my loved ones, including our kids, while I watched and then killing me."*

Surprisingly enough, the fear of my loved ones being harmed or killed before he killed me was the fear that called me into action.

When my only concern was about myself and no one else, I thought I could handle it. However, when the psychologist presented me with the multi-murder-suicide scenario, my whole outlook immediately took a one-hundred-and-eighty-degree turn. It ignited and flamed the fire of all my efforts to escape from the abusive relationship I had been imprisoned in. I had to protect my family and myself from harm.

To be fully transparent, the answers to the majority of my whys were based on pride, fear, shame, and my "I can do all things through Me, Myself and I" ego. But the biggest explanation for it all was that I felt guilty.

As you've already read, I believed and felt that I had brought it all upon myself. I deserved it because I had failed to stand strong in my faith during that pre-Thanksgiving weekend in Arkansas. I should have done and been better at not giving in to my worldly desires and ways.

Many times, I had asked God to forgive me. However, I hadn't truly accepted or believed the fact that He had. Therefore, I began living a life of self-condemnation, telling myself I'd failed and deserved everything that was happening to me. I had gotten lost in my own condemnation and had forgotten a very important Bible verse: "There is therefore, now no condemnation for those who are in Christ Jesus" (Romans 8:1, NKJ). And that "no" means none, zero, zilch!

As that thought profoundly penetrated my mind, I once again asked for the Lord's forgiveness. But this time, I fully claimed it and believed He had.

The Resolve

A peace that I couldn't explain grew within me as that verse sank deep within me. I realized that the devil knew me very well. He had used all my weaknesses and trigger points to keep me under his thumb to live a life full of self-condemnation and abuse. His tactics used against me had been strong. But I had come out on the other side and was now claiming my victory over him. I literally told the devil he didn't understand who he was dealing with anymore because the Bible says, Greater is He who is within me than he who is in the world! (1John 4:4, KJV)

That fact became clearer as I realized that almost everything in my life had or was about to change. I was no longer living in an abusive and fear-filled environment. It was gone. I was now living in a peaceful place where I had many opportunities to spend focused time with God. I was forgiven, free, full of hope, and moving forward. Something new was awaiting me!

> ***Words of Wisdom:*** *There's a verse in the Bible that, in reality, defines what it's like to live within an abusive relationship. It is found in 2 Corinthians 11:19–20 (NLT), and it states, "After all, you think you are so wise, but you enjoy putting up with fools! You put up with it when someone enslaves you, takes everything you have, takes advantage of you, takes*

control of everything, and slaps you in the face." When it comes to living within an abusive relationship, that definition hits the nail, smack dab, on the head. Therefore, if you are in an abusive relationship of any kind, please take the following scriptures to heart. Start believing them and take immediate action, implementing their truths into your life:

- *Philippians 1:28 (NLT) "Don't be intimidated in any way by your enemies. This will be a sign to them that they are going to be destroyed, but that you are going to be saved, even by God himself."*
- *2 Timothy 1:7 (NKJV) "For God has not given us a spirit of fear, but of power, love, and a sound mind."*
- *Joshua 1:9 (NLT) "Be strong and courageous! Do not be afraid or discouraged. For the Lord your God is with you wherever you go."*

- *1 John 3:20–22 "If our hearts condemn us, we know that God is greater than our hearts, and he knows everything. Dear friends, if our hearts do not condemn us, we have confidence before God and receive from him anything we ask, because we keep his commands and do what pleases him."*

- *Proverbs 3:5–6 "Trust in the Lord with all your heart and lean not on your own understanding; in all your ways submit to him, and he will make your paths straight."*

When you daily implement these verses into your life, God will prove that he keeps his promises. He can, wants to, and will do the same for you. And once you do, what will be the result of having done all of this? The answer is: "The God of hope will fill you with all joy and peace as you trust in him, so that you may overflow with hope by the power of the Holy Spirit." (Romans 15:13, NIV). Trust and obey His Word because it's true and He only wants the best for you. Hope, safety, happiness, and a future await you!

If you are presently living within an abusive relationship, please take the following to heart. Begin implementing these "Do's and Dont's" into your life and contact the resources I share with you. I did and that's why I'm living "free at last!"

- Realize escaping an abusive relationship is dangerous, and you can't do it by yourself. Therefore, don't keep it to yourself. Tell several people you trust and who truly care about you what is going on in your life. Build a caring support team that holds resources and the ability to provide the wise input and guidance you need. Realize there are people in your life who have some inkling that something is going wrong in your life, and they stand ready to help you if you ask for it. You'll experience the truth in the statement, "We're stronger together."

- Create a personal safety plan of action.
- Don't believe your abuser's lies. They know lies feed your fear. And what is FEAR? It is only "False Evidence Appearing Real!"
- Don't try to be your abuser's savior. There has only been one Savior, Jesus, and it will never be you or me.
- Don't let your present situation or circumstances dominate and rule over your future. Move forward!
- Choose God's faithfulness over your fears. Let God lead, guide, direct, love, and protect you. You just may see, He only wants the best-ever life for you and realize the new life that awaits you!
- If you or someone you know is in an abusive relationship, here are several things that you should do that will prove most beneficial to follow through with:
    - Conduct an online search for local resources available for the battered and abused.
    - Contact the National Domestic Violence Hotline by:
        - Dial 800–799–7233,
        - Text the word BEGIN to 8878,
        - Visit https://www.thehotline.org.

~ 15 ~
NEW LIFE TASKS, TROUBLES, AND TRIUMPHS

My new life brought major personal and professional tasks that needed to be accomplished. All of them brought their troubles along with them. The first two were connected directly to my personal life. The third was a multi-level task that was solely professionally oriented and demanded many hours of focused energy as the Center's special programs coordinator.

Personal Tasks

Task One

All the stuff in the townhouse had to be packed up and ready to hopefully move into my new home soon. The entire house had to be cleaned so it would be left spic and span and in better condition than it was originally. However, just in case a new home had not been secured by May 31st, I had to also be prepared to have it moved into a storage facility.

Thanks to the support of my sisters and their families, this was accomplished before the 31st.

Task Two

The search to find and secure a place I could call my own began on the same day as Task One. My goal was to have this accomplished by the end of May. In today's world, that task might not seem to be a difficult thing to do. However, at that time, it was challenging. The ease with which today's online search resources did not exist. Only two resources were available to me: rental listings in all the local newspapers and asking people in my life to let me know if they saw or heard of anything available.

There were six major concerns I held in finding and securing a new home. (a) It had to be affordable. Doug had burdened me with debt. I knew I could pay it off, but it would take time, and presently, money was tight. (b) Its location had to provide "easy on, easy off" access to the highways that would easily take me wherever I needed to go. (c) The Landlord had to have an understanding heart regarding the situation I had recently come out of. (d) Given my recent townhouse landlord experience, the new landlord had to show signs of taking care of the property and not needing my money any more than I did. (e) Having been a landlord myself in the past, I knew what having both good and bad tenants was like. (f) This item was essential and was daily lifted to the Lord—the landlord would understand what I meant when I told them that I didn't want to be their tenant, but I wanted to make their property my new forever home. (g) I wanted to secure it all by May 31st.

Two-fold Task Three—Taking Care of Business

The first day back to work after moving into Jo and Ken's former home started awesomely. I felt like everyone was welcoming me back from medical leave. However, as the day progressed, it became quite evident that I was back in the real Monday-through-Friday workaday world. Don't get me wrong, I had performed all required of me as I went through the past personally horrific four and a half months of my life. However, a special meeting with the Chamber's president, plus another special meeting with the OSBDC director, had been unexpectedly added to my first day of being "fully" back to work. By the end of the day, these meetings would assign me two new and significant business tasks. I remember thinking, *Now, not only do I need to find my new forever home but seriously focus my energies on completing two new business tasks.*

Business Task One

The Chamber president stated that he and the OSBDC director wanted me to, once again, coordinate all efforts to bring the Florida theme park's day-long professional development program back to Columbus. Their target time frame for holding the event would be sometime in September or October 2001. I had successfully done so in 2000, and they knew I could do it again.

However, what neither he nor the Center's director knew was that I had begun working to develop and secure everything well over eight months before the mid-September 2000 event was successfully held. The Florida theme park had mandatory contracts, time frames, rules, regulations, marketing standards, event facility requirements, mandated minimum registration fees, and guaranteed attendance requirements. It all had to adhere to a T, or it would be a "no-go" situation. It was now June 2001, and I had only four months left to complete what had previously taken me eight months. Time was of the essence, and there was a great deal to accomplish within a limited timeframe.

The stress of it all began to build within me as the meeting ended. As I left the meeting and headed to meet with my boss, my mind started compiling a lengthy list of things that had to be done immediately, and I began silently praying, *Oh Lord, help me. Help me now.*

Business Task Two

The focused topics discussed during the meeting with my boss were the past efforts and plans being laid to revitalize the Small Business Administration's (SBA) Women's Network for Educational Training (WNET) program for the Center. It was a mentoring program that paired an existing woman business owner with a woman wanting to start her own business. My boss was relentless and wanted it to happen. My report and input were as follows.

From day one, I had tried to explain to my boss that this program, which had been promoted by the Small Business Administration (SBA) since the early 80s, was now antiquated. It wasn't meeting the needs held by today's existing women business owners or budding entrepreneurs.

In the process of promoting the program, a multitude of women business start-ups and a handful of existing women business owners became my clients. This made the boss happy. However, every start-up effort was requesting a business mentor, and few, if any, existing women business owners were willing to commit their time to serve in this capacity.

Therefore, all attempts to revive the outdated program had proven sorely unsuccessful.

I continued to report that in mid-2000, I had initiated a promotional and research plan to determine exactly why this program was no longer effective and to understand what the woman business owner and budding entrepreneur wanted in such a program.

This plan included attending monthly meetings and presenting the WNET mentoring program to the multitude of Women in Business organizations within the Center's eight-county service area. The information was well received, and many existing women business owners gave me their business cards, stating they would be in touch, and many of them did.

However, when they called, none of them wanted to be a mentor. Instead, they wanted a mentor. Therein lay the problem. Something new was needed, and it had to meet the needs of both start-up and existing women business owners. They all wanted to learn and have a mentor while they did so. Therefore, by the end of 2000, I had begun working on the challenge of developing such a program. However, my private life during the first five months of 2001 had put a slight damper on all these efforts.

Thankfully, my boss understood, but as our meeting ended, she strongly encouraged me to diligently work on it because she wanted it up and running by the end of the year.

I now had to successfully bring the Florida program to Columbus within four months, completely develop a new women in business program by the end of the year, maintain and care for all my existing one-on-one business advisory clients, and personally find a place to call my own home.

Piece of cake, right? *Not!* All of a sudden, my to-do plate was piled high and spilling all over me. I felt overwhelmed, pressured, worried, stressed, and extremely tired just thinking about these new demands, now added to all my other existing responsibilities.

As I left the office that night, a Scripture verse unexpectedly came into my mind. It was a verse I had memorized years ago. In this verse, Jesus was speaking to those who were feeling the same way I was. And Jesus told them, "Come to me, all you who are weary and heavy burdened, and I will give you rest" (Matthew 11:28).

Words cannot explain how glad I was that I'd memorized that verse, for great peace came over me in that moment. I instantly knew there were three essential things I needed to do as soon as I got home. If I hadn't, I wouldn't have successfully navigated it all.

I needed to rest my mind and weary spirit in Him. Next, I needed to pray, believing He would answer me. And finally, yet most importantly, I needed to purposefully reclaim and reestablish the same daily devotional time with God and delving into His Word that I had while living at CHOICES. Therefore, that's exactly what I did. I needed the rest, peace, strength, wisdom, and guidance that only He could provide. These things were the only things that could help meet these new demands and stay sane while getting through them all. I couldn't do it without Him.

Words of Wisdom: *If you are carrying an impossibly heavy burden and trying to manage its enormous load all by yourself, do the most important thing that you could ever do. Ask God for help and surrender it all to Him. Yes, there will still be plenty of work to be done, but you won't be doing it* *alone. He knows what's going on better than you do. He also knows how best to handle everything. Let Him teach you, lead you, direct you, and open doors for you that no man can shut and close doors that no one can open. You have an all-powerful God who makes impossible things possible. Draw close to the One who will lead, guide, and direct each step you take. He longs for you to give your burdens to Him. He wants you to come close to Him, fall in step beside Him, lean on Him, and trust Him because He truly cares for you. Therefore, don't rely on yourself. Rely on God. The One who never fails or leaves you. He's the one who will give you rest, peace, strength, and the guidance you need. Do your best as He directs and let Him do all the rest. Why? Because when you do, you'll thrive in life, at work, and in all you do.*

Triumphs

Here's how the Lord first showed up. It was less than a week after implementing all of the above. It happened one night as I thought about the small group Bible study I had just attended at church. People of all ages had been present. Each of them held different levels of spiritual growth, understanding, and experiences. The night had been filled with great insights, sharing, and learning.

Everyone present had walked away with something new to think about or implement into their lives.

There it was! I could utilize this small group concept to establish the new women's business development program. It would bring together budding women entrepreneurs and existing women business owners to learn from and share their resources and experiences. Over time, they would become mentors to one another.

The Lord helped me identify exactly how to lay the foundation upon which to build and create the new women in business mentoring program for the Center. Now, all I had to do was meticulously design and establish all the program's operational format, secure the best place to hold monthly meetings, recruit expert guest speakers, develop the marketing message, define and decide where and how best to promote the program to its target market, and finally, launch the program by the end of 2001. Yes, my plate was still full, and my workload was still considerable. But thanks be to God! He was leading and guiding me all the way!

The next triumph initially felt like anything but a triumph. But wait for it. The Lord tells us to wait while He goes before us. So, wait for it. He's working even when we can't see it, and His timing is perfect. So wait as I did . . . it's coming!

My spirit and my heart were crushed when finding a home to call my own was not met by my deadline date of May 31st. Ya wanna talk about crying prayers of "Why, Lord, why?" They flowed like mighty rivers.

My family helped me move all my stuff into a storage unit. The upstairs level of Jo's former home continued to serve as my temporary home as I continued my search for a new, forever home. However, as May flowed into June, I calmed down and began to thank God for still having a safe place to live, at no cost, until I did find my new home.

The final walk-through of the townhouse was held with my former landlord, and he refused to refund my security deposit. His refusal to do so was based on the damages he pointed out and accused me of causing to the property.

Oh, he fully didn't understand who he was dealing with! I've often told my friends, "You can mess with me all you want. But, honey, let me tell you, if you mess with my nest (meaning my family or my money), you'll have a fight on your hands." As I left the property and headed for my car, I quietly said to myself, "Oh, the fight is on! And in the end, you will refund me my deposit!"

You see, I am the type of person who keeps excellent records of everything. I had taken pictures of all pre-existing damage discovered during the initial walkthrough. I had also noted them on the property's floor plan of the property. Every damage he accused me of was pre-existing. Therefore, the very next day, and thanks to the connections I had at the Chamber, I contacted one of the attorneys who was a volunteer OSBDC advisor. After sharing everything and providing him with proof of my innocence, he agreed to send a nasty letter to my former landlord, threatening to file suit against him if he failed to refund the security deposit.

Almost immediately after receiving this notice, my former landlord contacted the attorney to advise that he would mail the check within the next two weeks.

Yes, that was a triumph. But wait! There's even more to the story because God's way is perfect and so is His timing. He proved it to me because early on during those two weeks of waiting, something wonderful happened.

Jo called my office and told me that there was a new 'for rent by owner' listing in the Grove City newspaper. Since she and Ken now lived in Grove City, she urged me to check it out. She gave me the address and all the necessary contact information if I were interested in making it my new home. And as she hung up, she enthusiastically said, "Oh my goodness, Nancy, we could soon be living in the same town and on Sundays, attend the same church once again!"

I called the number immediately and spoke to George, the property owner. During our conversation, I not only expressed my interest in scheduling a walk-through of the property but also provided him with a brief overview of my past and present circumstances that had led me to search for a new home.

There was a brief pause after I had shared my information, and my mind started to yell, "Oh, Nancy, you've shared too much!" But after his pause, the words he spoke surprised me as he said, "You are the first to call and request a viewing. My wife, Mary, has been listening to our conversation, and we both totally understand. We're both so sorry for what you've been through over the past several months. However, we both think that this is amazing! Are you available to come see the property tomorrow night? If so, let's get it scheduled, and while we show you the property, we'll also tell you why we think it's so amazing." The walkthrough was scheduled, directions to the property were given, and we all agreed we were looking forward to tomorrow.

I called my sister immediately after hanging up. I wanted to fill her in on my call and the amazing conversation that had just happened. We were both excited. Plans were made to stop by her house after the upcoming walkthrough. And as I hung up, a request for her prayer coverage was made over it all.

Anticipation of what tomorrow would bring began to build within me the moment I hung up the phone. What would the place look like? What amazing things would the property owners share with me? I wanted to go right then and there, but I was at work and had a workshop to conduct that night. I had to do something that I disliked doing. I had to wait! However, that night I prayed, "Lord, if this house is to be my new home, let it shout out my name! Let there be no question about it."

Tomorrow turned into today. I waited throughout the day, anticipating the clock to hit 5:00 p.m.

As soon as it did, I was out the door heading for Grove City. I was vaguely familiar with this community because, back in 1984, it had served as my home base during a three-month retail experience where I remerchandised the layout of multiple stores in the area. But during that time, all I was truly familiar with were the main thoroughfares, and that was seventeen years ago.

Grove City had changed. Gone was the affordable three-story hotel that my retail remerchandising team and I had lived in for three months in 1984. A Speedway gas station and convenience store now stood where it once was.

Economic development was thriving within the community. However, it still held that quaint conservative hometown environment and mindset. It was definitely "The best-kept secret in

Central Ohio," and offered easy-on-easy-off access to the Interstate highways that could take you anywhere, including downtown Columbus.

Following the directions provided to me, I turned into the neighborhood. I couldn't believe it. This couldn't be right. I must have incorrectly written down the directions or address. This neighborhood was too nice, and there were no rent signs in front of any house.

There was a police car parked in the driveway across the street, and a man was busy working in its yard, so I decided to stop and ask him where this address was. He replied, "It's right behind you. The owners are coming later tonight to put up the 'For Rent' sign. Might you be my new neighbor?" My reply was, "Oh, I hope and pray so! We've scheduled a six o'clock walkthrough of the property tonight." During the brief conversation that followed, he shared that he was a third-shift Grove City Police officer, had lived in the home behind him for many years, and loved the neighborhood, as well as Grove City.

As he turned to go inside to get ready for work, he wished me well and stated the property owners were good people and that he thought I'd like them. And as he disappeared, my mind was busy checking off some of my next-home-must-have things on the list.

I parked my car in front of the house and sat there waiting for about five minutes. Then it happened. A beautiful red Chevy Corvette pulled into the driveway. A very nicely dressed middle-aged man, George, and his wife, Mary, got out of the car. They turned, looked at me as if to say, "Are you Nancy?" and I nodded. They smiled and motioned for me to come. And as I did, my mind said, *Well, Lord, they don't need my money any more than I do! Check that one off my list as well. Lord, now I'm really getting excited! Let's go look at the house and listen to what they want to share with me.*

We didn't immediately enter the house, though. Instead, George had gotten three folding parade chairs out of the car and invited us all to sit on the front porch for a moment. The reason for the momentary delay was that he and Mary wanted to share why they both thought my call and interest in renting the property was amazing. As they shared the following, the excitement within me began to build even stronger:

- They had rented the property for over seven years to the same husband and wife.
- Their rent payments were never late and were always received in the mail a week before being due.
- The tenant never called about any concerns or about repairs needing to be done. And when George or Mary called, they always said everything was fine.

- Thinking all things were good, George and Mary only drove by the property, and everything always looked good.
- However, little did they know that even though the rental agreement states "No Pets," their tenants had purchased two Mastiff dogs during the second year of renting the property. The dogs were seldom let outside because they didn't want the neighbors to know, for fear that they would call George on them.
- During the weekend prior to the Thanksgiving holiday weekend, George received a call from one of the handymen he contracts with. The contractor wanted to know when George last visited the property. George told him it had been years since his tenants had always reported that all was good and they had never had any complaints. His contractor then instructed him to check it out immediately. The contractor had just been there to perform a minor repair requested by the tenant. The repair was done and paid for, but the entire interior of the house, all three floors, was a total disaster area. The entire house was worse than badly damaged, and it smelled like dog urine and feces.
    - My mind shouted, *Oh my gosh, Lord, that's the weekend I was in Arkansas, and when all my troubles truly began!*
- George and his wife immediately visited and found all the handyman's reports to be terribly true.

- They evicted the tenant the day before New Year's Eve
    - My mind yelled, *Oh my gosh! Lord, that's the day Doug showed up at my door and reentered my life.*
- The total rehab and restoration of the entire house began a week after the eviction.
- They wanted it completed by May 31st but failed to meet that deadline. However, a week ago, it was all completed. The whole house had been renovated and made brand new, and was now ready to be rented to someone who truly needs it and would take care of it as if it were their own.
    - This time, my mind humbly thought, *Oh Lord, May 31st was also my deadline date for finding a new home. I think you're also trying to tell me that George understood it when I told him I didn't want to be his tenant but wanted to make his property my home. Lord, I also think you're trying to show me that even though I didn't know it, you've been working all things for my good.*

My focus returned to the present as I heard George say, "Well, Nancy, are you ready to go inside for your walkthrough and see what we've done?"

My immediate reply was, "Yes, please!" And as soon as I walked in, it was as if it shouted my name, and I heard a small, quiet voice inside me say, *Nancy, this is your new home!*

George and Mary guided me through a comprehensive tour of the split-level, three-bedroom, one-and-a-half-bath home. Everything was brand new and beautifully done. It had everything I needed. Its lower level would even fulfill one of my heart's desires, as it could easily accommodate a billiard table when I could afford a used one. No other place I'd looked at during my search for a new home came close to meeting this desire. This one exceeded them all!

Why did I hold this heart's desire? I absolutely loved shooting pool. It had become my only hobby. However, the Bible instructs us many times to take control of our thoughts and to be cautious in the choices we make about where we go and with whom we associate. For whom you hang with, you become. And my entire life, let alone the past five months of my life, had taught me the importance of adhering to this Godly advice.

Therefore, I didn't want to go to a bar or billiards parlor anymore because it might put me, once again, in a place that would obstruct my ability to make the right choices, hinder me, and weaken my walk with God. I wanted nothing in my life that might cause me to mess up again in any way, shape, or form. I didn't want anything to distract me from focusing on God and His will for my life.

In addition to all of this, I didn't want to do anything that might cause someone to wrongly brand me as a Christian hypocrite if they saw me going into a bar. They wouldn't know that all I wanted or intended to do was to shoot a couple of rounds of pool and leave. I wanted to avoid letting any negative aspects return to my life. All I wanted was to avoid any worldly temptations and become a faithful follower of Christ, both publicly and privately.

Therefore, George and Mary's property would more than meet all of my desires. The whole place was too good to be true. But it was!

After the walkthrough, we all went back out and sat on the front porch. There, George reviewed the rental agreement, the upfront security fee, and the monthly rental fee. I found both astonishingly affordable. With all things covered, George ended it all by saying, "Nancy, we have been working on this property since the beginning of the year. We were going to sell it but decided to spend the money to rehab it and make it all brand new for our next tenant. The last five months have been tough on us. But we've gotten through them all."

"Nancy, you, too, have been through an unspeakable ordeal over the past five months. Nothing like ours, but they've both been tough on both sides of our fences. And look, we've all gotten through them for the better."

"This place is, literally, ready to move in. And we want to rent it to you as soon as possible because we believe the good Lord sent you to us. But first, and just to be safe, we need to check your reference. We're sure they'll all check out. So, here's what we'd like to propose. Have your security deposit and your prorated first month's rent ready in a couple of days. We'll give you a call as soon as your references are checked and set up a time for you to come sign the rental agreement. We want you to live here and take care of this property as though it were your own. Mary and I truly believe God is at work and is working for the good in all of our lives."

I joyfully agreed with them in all things as I stood to leave and told them I would be looking forward to hearing from them soon. I hopped into my car and immediately headed for Jo's. I couldn't wait to share all that had just happened. And as I did, the praise and excitement within both of us continued to grow as we rejoiced in the Lord for how He was working in my life.

Two days later, all monies were ready and waiting for George's call. It took almost all of my savings to do it. Therefore, my budget for the coming months would be tight.

However, the very next day, two more triumphant things happened. First, George called me to confirm it was a go! A time to meet that night was set to determine a move-in date, sign the rental agreement, and pay all necessary fees to make it happen.

Yes, that was a triumph. But wait! Here's triumph number two that once again proved God's timing is perfect!

Remember that check my former landlord said he'd send to my attorney? Well, he did, and my attorney personally delivered it to me that same afternoon. Plus, my attorney did not charge me a single penny for his services in helping me! The check was deposited into my bank account, and all my financial concerns were washed away. That night, George and I met. All business was taken care of, and all payments were made in full. I would be able to move into my new home the following week.

A great troop of family and friends, with their able bodies, vans, and trucks, all rallied to my call for help moving. And the move-in of all my "stuff", although not yet fully unpacked, was completed by Saturday, June 16th.

The first night in my new home was filled with thoughts about how God had taken care of me over the past five and a half months. My mind was filled with amazement. I saw how He had been with me, working for me, and getting me safely through it all. I praised Him for how, from day one, He had gone before me to prepare the 'brand new' home, connecting me to it, and had worked out every detail to assure it would be mine.

How it all happened amazed me. Once again, God did it all. His timing in all things was perfect. And my new home was above and beyond what I could have ever asked for or imagined. The only thing I did or had to do was follow through when He opened the door of opportunity.

That night, as I crawled into bed, He had proven that He answers my prayers. He had verified that His ways were better than mine. And He showed me that He takes better care of me than I could ever take care of myself. Yes, the search for a new home was completed. I even had a new home church that I would attend with my sister.

However, as I tried to drift off to sleep, my new work demands began to fill my mind. Stress began to build. In response to this, I began to pray. I reaffirmed my commitment to spending daily time purposefully delving into His Word and praying with Him. I knew I couldn't do it without Him. "God Time" and His Word were needed to help me meet the demands, stay sane, and accomplish them all.

Words of Wisdom: *Remember these verses when you feel overwhelmed, worried, and exhausted just thinking of all that must be done in meeting the demands and expectations that this world puts upon you. Hide them in your heart. Remember them. Believe them. They were the peace-giving and strength-building nuggets God shared with me over the weeks and months to* *come. They will strengthen and support your efforts to maintain a spirit of inner peace when life's demands seem to be crashing down upon you.*

- *Matthew 11:28–29 "Come to me, all you who are weary and burdened, and I will give you rest. Take my yoke upon you and learn from me, for I am gentle and humble in heart, and you will find rest for your souls".*
- *1 Peter 5:7 "Cast all your anxiety on him because he cares for you."*
- *Psalm 23:1–3 "The Lord is my shepherd, I lack nothing. He makes me lie down in green pastures, he leads me beside quiet waters, he refreshes my soul. He guides me along the right paths for his name's sake."*
- *Psalm 121:5 (NLT) "The LORD himself watches over you! The LORD stands beside you as your protective shade."*
- *Hebrews 13:5b "God has said, 'Never will I leave you, never will I forsake you.'"*
- *Philippians 4:19 "And my God will meet all your needs according to the riches of his glory in Christ Jesus."*
- *Psalm 55:22 "Cast your cares on the LORD and he will sustain you; he will never let the righteous be shaken."*
- *Psalm 68:19 "Praise be to the Lord, to God our Savior, who daily bears our burdens."*
- *Exodus 14:14 "The Lord will fight for you; you need*

only to be still."

- *Romans 8:31 "What, then, shall we say in response to these things? If God is for us, who can be against us?"*
- *Isaiah 41:10 (NLT) "Don't be afraid, for I am with you. Don't be discouraged, for I am your God. I will strengthen you and help you. I will hold you up with my victorious right hand."*
- *Isaiah 40:29 "He gives strength to the weary and increases the power of the weak.*
- *Joshua 1:9 "Have I not commanded you? Be strong and courageous. Do not be afraid; do not be discouraged, for the LORD your God will be with you wherever you go."*
- *Proverbs 3:5-6 "Trust in the LORD with all your heart and lean not on your own understanding; in all your ways submit to him, and he will make your paths straight."*
- *Romans 8:28 "And we know that in all things God works for the good of those who love him, who have been called according to his purpose."*

Yes, my new work burdens were heavy, "But God" (those are two of my favorite words in the Bible) was with me all the way. And here's the proof.

During the following month, two unbelievable things happened regarding the Florida program. First, thanks to the past extreme success that both the Florida organization and the Chamber had experienced, the Florida leadership showered me with grace. They accepted my plea to waive their deadline date, and all paperwork was completed to seal the deal. Therefore, they would once again come and present their program in mid-October 2001.

Here's the other amazing thing that happened. Once this news hit the Chamber's and SBDC's committee grapevine, every committee chairman and committee member who had helped make the 2000 event a success called me. All of them confirmed their desire and intent to work on making the 2001 event an even greater success.

By the end of the month, not only was the event confirmed, but an experienced volunteer committee workforce was all in place. Now, that had to be God at work for me! Now, all I had to do was coordinate and orchestrate the effort to ensure all Florida requirements were met.

Yes, every victory won is the result of meeting a challenge and winning a battle. And the efforts to establish a new "Women in Business" program were both of these things and still present in my life.

The challenge of creating something new and entirely different was still staring me in the face. But thanks to the "Church Small Group" concept, the Lord had given me the plans were moving forward. However, it was not done.

Basic programmatic plans had been outlined, some contacts made, and several meetings had been held with a select small group of leading women business owners to obtain their insights and input. The work was all, "Under Construction." However, I was determined to fight the good fight and do everything necessary to meet my boss's December deadline for launching it.

The battle was to get it presented, explained, and approved by my boss once all this was completed. The trouble was that her mind was firmly set on resurrecting the WNET program. It was as though she had temporarily lost her hearing every time I approached the subject.

Given all that was on my plate, there was still much to be done, challenges to meet, and much to accomplish. However, I never lost sight of the fact that God was with me and would lead and guide me through it all. And that He did!

Time passed, and the new proposed Women in Business program was ready to be presented to my boss. Her first reply after my presentation was, "What about WNET?"

Once again, I stressed that the WNET program wasn't working. We had tons of women who wanted to start a business. However, there were few, if any, existing business owners willing to serve as a personal mentor to them. I also pointed out the fact that this was the reason my client case load was jammed with women wanting to start a business.

Something new had to take its place. However, she didn't like the idea at all. In her adamant opinion, having a mixture of existing and start-up business owners in the same room talking about business would not meet the mentorship purpose of WNET. She couldn't grasp the concept of group mentoring, wherein multiple levels of understanding and expertise come together to learn, provide insights, and share resources with one another.

I sat there feeling wounded but not defeated as she said, "I will not approve what you've proposed. However, since we have numerous women who desire to start a business but lack mentors, what would your next proposal be, given that I grant you a second chance?

Quietly sitting there for several lengthy moments, I prayed, *Oh my gosh, Lord, give me the words to say.* And my reply astounded me as I said, "Well, why don't you give me that second chance and a couple of days and see what I will propose. She agreed and scheduled a follow-up meeting for two days later.

Several days later, my presentation began by saying, "You know the 'E' and 'T' in WNET stand for Entreprenuerial Training. Why don't we establish a monthly educational class for our women's business startup clients? These classes would not only train in the basics of starting a business but also feature existing women business owners as special guest speakers. Their presentations would address a given business topic, issue, or even provide a list of dos and don'ts when starting a business. We could promote it as "The New WNET with a tagline something like, "Where Your Startup Education Thrives." Our first targeted market would be our existing women startup clients. However, once well-established, expand the promotional efforts to the general business public.

My boss was elated and loved it. She approved the idea immediately. I sat there thinking, "Thank you, Jesus! That was amazing and simple. But I'm keeping my first proposal close at hand. I know you gave that one to me as well. I know it will work in the future."

> ***Words of Wisdom:*** *When something wonderful happens in your life or an awesome resolution to a monumental problem comes to you, never think that it all happened from what you did. Instead, realize that it was a gift from God, for James 1:17 says, "Every good and perfect gift is from above, coming down from the Father." God made it happen and gave it to you as a wonderful and awesome gift. Then, from your heart, give Him praise and thanks for it.*

The whole day had turned out to be fabulous. Traveling home, even the downtown and interstate traffic turned out to be trouble-free. As I took the Grove City exit off of SR270, I remember thinking, *Lord, it's been a wonderful day. I'm heading home for a peaceful night in the home you gave me and that I now call my home. It can't get any better than this.*

But something even more amazing was about to happen. I'll never forget it.

My dear reader, let me pause for a moment and ask you a question. Have you ever experienced something incredible happening in just a few seconds, and within those seconds, many different thoughts have flowed through your mind? Therefore, when you tried to tell someone about it, it took more than several minutes to do so. Well, here's mine. But please read on. It will be well worth your reading!

As I turned left onto the road that would lead me to my new home, I looked up and saw the overhead road sign indicating the name of the road. The sign read "HOME." It was at that very moment that I heard a quiet voice inside me say, *Nancy, remember that night in Texas when you cried to Me and asked Me to show you where home was? Well, here it is. You are home.*

But wait! It gets better!

Tears of joy started to flow down my cheeks. To assure I wasn't causing any traffic problems, I quickly checked my rearview mirror. The Speedway gas station filled the mirror. Far behind it was a massive and extremely tall security fence, thickly covered with overgrown weeds and shrubbery. But that was not what truly caught my eye. My attention was drawn to something you really wouldn't notice if you didn't know what it was or if it once existed. I saw the third floor of the hotel, in which my remerchandising crew and I had occupied five rooms seventeen years earlier. It was now vacant, dilapidated, abandoned, and condemned for destruction.

My first thought was, *Oh, how sad. Many memories were made within those walls.* However, that thought was quickly replaced with an unbelievable yet true memory. It was the memory of the night I had left the hotel to explore Grove City. And, as I did, I fell in love with the town and told God that I wouldn't mind living in Grove City someday. As that memory flashed through my mind, I yelled, "Oh my gosh, Lord, that was seventeen years and many places ago! You heard me then, and that 'someday' is now!"

My heart was jumping for joy, and my body was covered in goose bumps as I entered my beautiful, brand-new home. It was the home that God had started preparing for me over nearly eighteen years ago.

All my thoughts that night were not only focused on the past seven months, but also on my entire life. I humbly thanked God for never abandoning me, always loving me, and showering me with His mercy and glorious grace in every good, bad, and downright ugly moment of it. He had taken care of me and been faithful to me even when I wasn't faithful to Him. He unconditionally loved me through it all and made it all work for my good! He had even worked on it to bring me back to Grove City! How cool was that?!

The thought of His love for me was overwhelming me. Tears, once again, welled up in my eyes. My heart felt like it was filled and overflowing with love for Him. He loved me in all my messes and troubles. My newfound awareness of His unconditional love sparked a deeper desire to love and serve Him.

From the depths of my heart, I prayed, *Lord, the words in my brain cannot express how much I love You. You are my everything. I want to live a godly Christ-centered life. I love You! I want to live my life for your glory, not mine. I want to serve and seek You first in all I do and say. Teach me how to trust You in all things, no matter what those things are. Help strengthen my efforts to renew my mind. Show me how to apply Your Word in my life. I surrender it all to You. Lord, I want to live for, love, and serve You with all my heart, soul, mind, and strength. I want to trust You in all things. Help me become the person You have designed me to become. Work through me and with me so that, by Your strength, the plan You have for me will be accomplished. Here I am, Lord. I love You with all my heart. In Jesus' name, Amen, and let it be done.*

As I said "Amen," my thoughts went back to my last night at CHOICES when I heard a quiet voice say, *Be still and know that I am God. Get ready! I'm about to do a New Thing!*

I instantly knew, without a doubt, that "new thing" was so much more than simply giving me a new home in a town that I loved. That "new thing" was my new life, living in and for Him.

With humble tears pouring out from my heart and flowing down my face, I shouted to the Lord, "Here I am, Lord. I'm ready and totally Yours! Your 'new thing' is the kind of life I want to live. Please, lead, guide, and direct me, for I know we, together, can make it happen! Let's do it!"

> **Words of Wisdom:** *We all experience troubles and storms in our lives. However, it's what we do within them that determines how or if we move forward through them. We can choose to throw down the towel, complain, and remain within them. Or we can press into God's power, strength, and guidance to move us forward, grow from them, and see what He has in store for us on the other side of it all. Move forward and walk through it with God. That is what King David did when he said, "Yea, though I walk through the valley of the shadow of death, I will fear no evil, for You are with me. Your rod and Your staff, they comfort me"(Psalm 23:4, NKJV).*

Yes, sometimes life is hard, and it hurts, but always remember one of the key words you just read was "through." Keep going! Move forward. See every crisis in your life as an opportunity to learn, press into God's Word, and increase your faith to trust in Him. You'll see Him move on your behalf, and you'll come out even better on the other side of it all with a stronger faith and trust in Him.

EPILOGUE

My growth in and love for God deepened greatly. It wasn't just because He had resolved all my dangerous, painful, and difficult situations. More importantly, it was because through them all He had shown and taught me how His power worked within my life and through it all. Therefore, I became even more self-aware of His awesome power at work in my life. And my life's view took a 180-degree turn in a loving direction as a result.

Fervent vigor filled me as my new life in Him began. Every morning, I stood in awe of how He had worked and was working in my life. The growing desire to love and serve Him fueled all I did.

Attending Sunday Contemporary Worship services with my sister became a regular thing. I loved listening to and was spiritually strengthened by every word Ken shared with his congregation and me. I absolutely loved my church family and sharing life with them all.

As time passed, I became actively involved in the church, serving as a member of the Contemporary Praise and Worship Team and as the well-known "Sucker Lady," joyfully giving Blow Pop suckers to all the children after church.

I woke up each workday morning eager to go to work and utilize the talents, skills, and abilities He had blessed me with. And each night, I praised Him for establishing me in a city I absolutely loved. He was proving to me that He only wanted the best for me. He was meeting all my needs and even fulfilling some of my heart's desires!

Still, I knew He wasn't done with me. He had more in store for me. Therefore, I would soon learn that I had more to learn and apply to my life. I had to daily renew my thoughts to get them in sync with His. I had to change my desires into His to fully begin living my new life. His desires and ways needed to become mine. His words needed to blend with mine. Why? Because I wanted to become stronger, more focused on becoming who He truly wanted me to be. After all, wasn't that what transformation is all about?

However, still being somewhat of a control freak at that time in my life, I soon would find that I was much like the apostle Paul when he said, "I do not understand what I do. For what I want to do I do not do, but what I hate I do" (Romans 7:15).

I truly didn't know or understand the challenges I would face in making my transformation happen. Therefore, some of my future worst internal troubles and frustrations were those I'd bring upon myself. And oh, I had them.

Dear reader, I would like to bring two important points to your attention right now. Your salvation in Christ is instantaneous! When you declare and believe that Jesus is God's Son, that He died on the cross and rose again to save you, and ask for His forgiveness of all your sins, you're saved! It's a gift freely given to you. All you have to do is truly accept it, believe it, and instantaneously you're a member of God's family!

On the other hand, meeting the challenges to renew your mind to align with His is a totally different, never-ending story. Renewing your mind and becoming sanctified isn't a quick, easy, one-and-done task. It's a daily, minute-by-minute task that leads to living a better life, the new life God designed for you to live.

My "totally different, never-ending story" will be shared in my upcoming third book entitled, "Praise God He Knew the Challenges I'd Face." It will hold stories of all the frustrations, troubles, tears, and triumphs experienced in meeting the many transformational challenges I'd face. And believe me, those challenges weren't easy. Many of them I still face today. However, the victories achieved in meeting the challenge were truly triumphant!

In the meantime, take a moment to reflect on your current life and circumstances. Are there bad habits, hurts, or hatred that you're holding onto that you would be hesitant to surrender to Jesus? Are there things that serve your own desires rather than God's? Are there relationships that need to be either strengthened or let go? Do you want to change?

If you do, remember you must first change the way you think.

Whatever your responses are, remember these truths found in Psalm 46:1 and Nahum 1:7:

God is your strength and refuge in times of trouble.

God cares for you when you love and trust in Him.

God is good!

www.ingramcontent.com/pod-product-compliance
Lightning Source LLC
LaVergne TN
LVHW050623100826
845148LV00011B/1705
* 9 7 9 8 9 8 6 9 1 9 6 2 1 *